Fitness Walking

Second Edition

Therese Iknoian

Human Kinetics

Library of Congress Cataloging-in-Publication Data

Iknoian, Therese, 1957-
    Fitness walking / Therese Iknoian. – 2nd ed.
        p.   cm.
    Includes index.
    ISBN 0-7360-5608-4
    1. Fitness walking.   I. Title.
    RA781.65.I39   2005
    613.7'176–dc22

                                    2004026209

ISBN: 0-7360-5608-4

Acquisitions Editor: Jana Hunter; **Developmental Editor:** Anne Cole; **Assistant Editors:** Wendy McLaughlin and Kim Thoren; **Copyeditor:** Annette Pierce; **Proofreader:** Erin Cler; **Indexer:** Bobbi Swanson; **Permission Manager:** Carly Breeding; **Graphic Designer:** Nancy Rasmus; **Graphic Artist:** Sandra Meier; **Photo Manager:** Dan Wendt; **Cover Designer:** Keith Blomberg; **Photographer (cover):** Comstock Images; **Photographer (interior):** Human Kinetics/Dan Wendt, unless otherwise noted; **Printer:** United Graphics

Human Kinetics books are available at special discounts for bulk purchase. Special editions or book excerpts can also be created to specification. For details, contact the Special Sales Manager at Human Kinetics.

Printed in the United States of America   10 9 8 7 6 5 4 3 2 1

Human Kinetics
Web site: www.HumanKinetics.com

United States: Human Kinetics
P.O. Box 5076
Champaign, IL 61825-5076
800-747-4457
e-mail: humank@hkusa.com

Canada: Human Kinetics
475 Devonshire Road Unit 100
Windsor, ON N8Y 2L5
800-465-7301 (in Canada only)
e-mail: orders@hkcanada.com

Europe: Human Kinetics
107 Bradford Road
Stanningley
Leeds LS28 6AT, United Kingdom
+44 (0) 113 255 5665
e-mail: hk@hkeurope.com

Australia: Human Kinetics
57A Price Avenue
Lower Mitcham, South Australia 5062
08 8277 1555
e-mail: liaw@hkaustralia.com

New Zealand: Human Kinetics
Division of Sports Distributors NZ Ltd.
P.O. Box 300 226 Albany
North Shore City
Auckland
0064 9 448 1207
e-mail: blairc@hknewz.com

Fitness Walking

Contents

Preface

Walking for fitness and health has become widely accepted since I wrote the first edition of this book nearly a decade ago. That was the era when most people overlooked the simple, enjoyable, *and effective* activity of fitness walking for controlling their health, fitness, or weight. It was just too, well, obvious. We were pounding ourselves silly in aerobics classes and feeling obligated to run (even if it didn't feel good) because we assumed those to be the best ways to get results.

Those who walked for fitness were considered second-class citizens. "Oh poor you, you can't run," "Oh, you must be too old for anything else," or "Gosh, can't you afford a gym?" Walking wasn't even surveyed until the mid-1980s by the sports data gurus who monitor the annual growth of fitness activities. What a relief that times have changed.

Today, more people walk—and proudly admit it—than participate in any other fitness activity in the United States. According to the Sporting Goods Manufacturers Association (SGMA), the number of people who count themselves as fitness walkers has grown nearly 40 percent since 1987. As of 2003, some 16.4 million call walking their primary mode of exercise, hitting their stride at least 100 days a year.

Of course, the popularity of treadmills used by many of those walkers has skyrocketed, and, although not officially surveyed, manufacturers and retailers know that most of these treadmill buyers are walkers. Since treadmills can be an excellent way to get in a workout, I've included some information about how to use one in your workout program.

Whether you're a beginner or have previous walking experience, whether you're old or young, or whether you intend to walk indoors on a treadmill or outside, this book shows you how to be successful.

Just toying with the idea of starting a walking program? I provide the basics to get you started and, most important, keep you injury free, motivated, and moving. Part I lays the foundation for step-by-step progress through health and walking evaluations, plus includes tips on how to dress, what to wear, and how to warm up and cool down. It also reviews key stretches. Although you learned to take your first steps as toddlers, proper fitness walking technique, reviewed in part I, can help you get more out of your workout and feel better, too.

Perhaps you've been tempted to walk for fitness, but you are already fit and feel you won't be able to elevate your heart rate to workout levels. Oh, not to worry! The technique review shows you how to move fast and fleet, using terrain and your body to get what you need. Part I also prepares you for outdoor workouts with discussions on apparel and gear for the trails and paths.

With the basics in hand, you next move on to part II and the menu of workouts. The 60 workouts are arranged by duration and intensity, making it easy for you to choose workouts suited to you. The sample programs in part III show you how to design your own program, using these workouts as a base. Part III also includes an extensive discussion of cross-training, with ideas for activities at various fitness levels.

And for those who are already walkers, I introduce the sport of race walking, an Olympic event that can be more physically demanding than running (I've had runners tell me they tried race walking but it was "too hard") and more mentally demanding than chess (mandatory focus on technique keeps your mind occupied and helps time fly). My book, *Walking Fast* (Human Kinetics, 1998), is an advanced walkers' guide and goes into more detail. Nevertheless, you can use the higher-level workouts in part II to dabble with faster-paced walking whether you want to race or not; the instructions for developing a program are a great first step for an advanced walker who wants more. The variety of cross-training ideas in part III help advanced walkers choose activities when they want a day off from walking.

Perhaps good or better health is the reason you're considering a walking program, or a stepped-up walking program. Many benefits of fitness walking fall outside the scientific framework; however, I believe your soul already knows these:

- **Walking is simple.** Although various gadgets and high-tech shoes and clothing can tickle your fancy, all you really need to walk is a pair of supportive shoes.

- **Walking travels well.** Whether you're at home, on vacation, or on a business trip, a walk is always just a step away. There's no need to worry about finding a certain environment (snow, water, smooth paths, hills, health clubs, or aerobics classes) for a workout.

- **Walking is social.** Walks are a great excuse to spend time visiting with friends or catching up with the family. Whether grandparents or grandkids, everyone can join in.

- **Walking is private.** Walking is also a great way to be by yourself and take a few deep breaths, release stress, think through problems or happiness, or just relax.

- **Walking is efficient.** Once you learn to use your legs and pump your arms, walking exercises both upper-body and lower-body muscles. Many other activities rely on only one part of the body.

The beauty of the first edition of *Fitness Walking* was its simplicity in presentation, style, and workouts. This second edition maintains that. I talk to you as if you're sitting on the couch with me. You won't find fancy scientific patter, although I certainly give you the basics you need to understand and appreciate what you're doing and how it can help you. You won't find convoluted programs but rather easy-to-follow workouts you can mix and match. This book is your mentor: a book that you may read sections of as you need them, refer to as a way to double-check what you're doing, or flip back through when you want to refresh your understanding of some aspect I've presented.

These days, when I look around on streets, tracks, or treadmills, it makes me smile to see 20-somethings striding out for fitness, even on college campuses. Seeing men walking brings me pleasure, too, because walking for so long was seen as an activity for women or, for goodness sake, older people. And hearing a runner espouse the beauty of cross-training with walking makes me smirk just a bit, too—sort of "I told you so." But I'd never say that.

Walking, you've come a long way, baby!

Acknowledgments

When I look back at the last two decades of being a walking advocate, teacher, mentor, and student, I see an amazing journey: from getting giggled at for believing in walking and being pitied (as if I chose walking because I couldn't do anything else) to finding that everyone suddenly wanted to be on the walking bandwagon and seeing walking devotees multiply.

My students over the years are the ones I admire for their devotion and thank for sharing many miles with me. I also thank the thousands upon thousands of readers of the first edition of this simple little book, which of course has made this second edition possible. They simply believed—believed in me and believed in what I and others said about the benefits of walking—and kept putting one foot in front of the other. Of course, I also remember with a smile and thank all the athletes, young and old, I've coached over the years. My biggest thanks goes to my young walking athletes. As young as 8 years old, they gave me the honor of watching them not only grow as walkers but also as people. I admire their maturity and thank them for all the lessons they unknowingly taught me. I also must thank my own mentors and supporters, particularly my original walking club, the Golden Gate Race Walkers, for being there, mile after mile, rain or shine, laughs or tears.

My husband, Michael, deserves more thanks than I can bestow in these few words. He has stood by my side and been one of my biggest fans. Ever patient, he puts up with my deadlines and makes me laugh when I most need it.

My parents, Richard and Roxy, deserve the biggest kudos. They have always supported me, listened to my dreams, and stood by my side, always willing to pick me up, dust me off, and shove me on my way again. I have been fortunate, indeed.

My thanks, love, and bear hugs to all.

The Essentials

Over the last decade, walking has solidly embedded itself into societies around the world, which has made it easier to call it what it is: walking. In fact, even in German, they use the English word to describe walking for fitness: *Ich gehe walking.* I loved seeing that for the first time on a club's bulletin board in Germany. So you're joining an international crowd with your choice of walking.

Nevertheless, you may have heard quite a few names for walking: power walking, striding, performance walking, aerobic walking, speed walking, fitness walking, sport striding, health walking, weight walking, and rhythm walking. And you've probably wondered if there's really a difference. In one study in the early 1990s, the researcher found 200 different names for walking! What a dilemma, you might think. Which type should I do? Am I an aerobic walker? Do I want to be a strider? Or perhaps I'm really more of a health walker.

Let's keep life simple. Walking is walking. Whether you're on your way to the car, heading around the block with the dog, or ready to do 4 miles on the local trail, it's all walking. You might go fast. You might go slow. Or you might go fast *and* slow. Maybe you add gadgets. Maybe you walk up hills, along city streets, or around the local mall. Whatever you do, the technique is the same. The only purpose for variations in arm position, foot placement, and leg or hip movement is to accommodate various speeds. The exception is race walking. When performed competitively, it is judged, and participants must follow rules or risk disqualification. Those rules, plus the speeds attained by race walkers, mandate a special technique, which I discuss briefly in chapter 2.

For our purposes in this book, I break down walking into four subcategories based on speed:

- **Health walking** is done at a slow pace and meant for beginners or for intermediate and advanced walkers doing an easy workout. Your heart rate will ease toward the low end of its training zone (see chapter 4 for details). Still, this is quicker than a window-shopping pace and can ease you into more vigorous walking if you're a beginner.

- **Fitness walking** is moving fast enough to raise your heart rate into its training zone. This means different speeds for different people, depending on their fitness levels. It can satisfy all fitness and health needs.

- **Athletic walking** begins to incorporate race-walking technique so you can pump along at a faster clip, raising your heart rate to the middle or top of your training zone. This level might be perfect for you if you want more challenge but don't want to bother with rules or take the step into competition. Athletic walking can also be used for speed play, where you alternate hard and easy periods in one workout.

- **Race walking** demands its own technique and can involve competitive racing with a training schedule similar to that of competitive runners. The emphasis is on improving performance, against yourself and others. You don't have to *race* to race walk, but if you compete, you must comply with rules, and you are judged.

No matter which of the four categories you think best describes the type of walking you want to do, part I shows you how to get started. Whatever your abilities and desires, you will improve your fitness, health, vigor, and longevity. Once you're immersed in a walking program, it's easy to become a disciple, preaching the joys of putting one foot in front of the other to everyone you meet. Walking offers a total package that's hard to beat. Once you're ready to give it a try, you can start out on the right foot by taking a closer look at walking's fitness and health benefits and how to evaluate your own level.

After reading part I, you will be able to pinpoint the type of walker you are and the type of program you need. You will also have a better understanding of how to improve your technique, warm up, cool down, and stretch. You'll also gain insights into how weather can affect a workout and how you feel, plus how to be safe, stay fueled, choose apparel and footwear, and how to measure the pace and distance of your walks. In fact, chapters 1 through 5 lay out the nuts and bolts of a walking program of any level in a way that will become a reference for years to come.

CHAPTER 1

Fitness Check

I doubt I need to convince you that walking can benefit your health. Thanks to research in the last decade, most people understand the benefits of walking. Since the first edition of this book, researchers have done substantial amounts of work on the topic of walking for fitness (not just performance or biomechanics). And as the buzz grew louder, what walkers have known all along was borne out scientifically: Regular walking will improve and maintain fitness and health.

Walking's Fitness Benefits

Walking affects the five components of fitness.

1. Body composition. Walking four times a week, 45 minutes each time, the average person can lose 18 pounds in a year with no change in diet, according to an early study at the University of Massachusetts Medical School. Key message: Walking can help you trim fat as well as tone your muscles.

2. Cardiovascular fitness. Walking, at any level or speed, two or three times a week for at least 20 minutes increases cardiovascular strength. Key message: By increasing the strength of your heart and lungs, you increase your ability not only to exercise longer and harder but also to perform everyday tasks without tiring.

3. Flexibility. As with any endurance activity, walking doesn't significantly increase your flexibility. Every activity uses certain muscle groups more than others. Therefore, if you don't stretch the muscles that walking uses extensively, they'll tighten, stay tight, and perhaps cause pains or strains. Key message: Flexibility exercises are still vital for remaining free of injury. Look for walking-specific flexibility exercises in chapter 5.

4. Muscular endurance. All walkers develop a moderate amount of endurance, which enables them to exercise longer before becoming exhausted. Race walkers have high endurance—comparable to that of marathon runners. Key message: Walking helps build your ability to do something longer without fatigue.

5. Muscular strength. You will gain muscular strength with walking but probably not enough for well-rounded fitness. Muscles that get an extra workout in walking include the entire back of the leg: calves, hamstrings, and gluteals

Walking can be both enjoyable and challenging.

(the buttocks). You'll also use muscles in the back and shoulders when you swing your arms. If you walk over hills, you may also develop more hip and thigh strength, and if you cross-train with other walking-oriented methods discussed in chapter 5, you may also develop additional back, chest, and arm strength. Key message: Walking strengthens targeted muscles, but doing specific exercises for other muscles will develop more balanced strength.

Walking provides other physical benefits and prevents dangers associated with other types of exercise. Walking is a low-impact exercise, which puts less strain on bones and tissues. Walkers land with one to one and a half times their body weight per foot strike, compared with three to four times for running. This creates less chance for injuries due to repetitive pounding.

Research indicates that walking helps bones stay strong and dense by forcing your body to bear its own weight. Although osteoporosis, a condition where bones become brittle, is a problem most common in older people, bone density can only be built and maintained when a person is young. Thin bones can lead to hip and spine fractures. A quarter of all women will ultimately fracture a hip, after which the average six-month survival rate is worse than after a heart attack. Men aren't immune to thin bones, either; they just get them later in life than women do.

Exercise will help build your immune system, too. In one study by Dr. David Nieman at Appalachian State University in North Carolina, a group of women who walked 45 minutes a day were half as likely to catch colds or flu than an inactive group. This immunity-boosting response applies to everyone, not just women.

Walking improves your spatial awareness and ability to balance because you balance on one foot with each step. The ability to avoid losing your balance, tripping, twisting an ankle, or falling requires control and training your proprioception—the ability of smaller muscles, such as those in your lower legs and ankles, to send accurate messages to nerves and other muscles to keep you upright. Although balance is something we take for granted, it takes training and practice, just like everything else.

From casual exercisers to Olympic athletes, walking offers everyone a challenge. Walking can be a slow stroll as you gain fitness, a dawdling saunter to spend time with the kids or to recover from injury, a daily fitness activity for life, or a high-level and challenging sport. Or it may be all of these for you, according to your mood or your energy level on a given day.

Evaluating Your Health and Fitness

Before you start a new activity program, even one as seemingly simple as walking, it's important to determine not only how healthy and fit you are in general but also how fit you are in the specific activity you want to begin. For example, if you are a very fit cyclist, you might not have the specific muscle

© Photodisc

From general fitness to preventing injuries, walking offers many health benefits.

strength or endurance for long or speedy walking workouts. On the other hand, even if you have been inactive for a while, you may have developed leg strength through everyday tasks such as gardening or dog walking, and you might not have to start with short and easy introductory workouts.

Remember, too, that healthy *and* fit don't always go hand in hand. You may be healthy in the medical sense (meaning you are free of clinical disease) but lack enough strength, flexibility, or endurance for physical activity. On the other hand, you might be strong from physical activity but show signs of disease because of genetics or poor lifestyle choices. Just because you are active doesn't mean you can eat all the junk you want or treat your body poorly. It *can* still talk back to you, and perhaps in ways you'd rather not hear.

No matter what your health and fitness levels or your current level of activity, it's important to reassess them prior to jumping into something new. Remember, the key to accurate results of any assessment is to be straightforward and honest in your answers. You'll only cheat yourself and your potential if you fib. In this case, a less-than-honest answer could also lead to injury rather than to maximum improvement and peak enjoyment of walking. And enjoyment is what we're after.

Although walking is a virtually injury-free sport, when you increase your activity level or try a different technique or new workout regimen, you suddenly put additional stress on a new part of your body or on previously unused muscles and tissues. While walking, it's still possible to aggravate an old injury you hadn't cared for properly or discover a genetic deficiency or muscle imbalance that was undetectable in your previous routine or because you were inactive.

As with any activity, be smart, ease into each new level, and listen to your body. This book will help you avoid the pitfalls and show you how to pace yourself as you progress. Be smart and be safe. That's the bottom line.

PAR-Q Test

The PAR-Q basic health screening, which stands for Physical Activity Readiness Questionnaire, is designed to set off alarm bells for high-risk conditions that need a doctor's consultation. It is only a general review. But don't blow it off as unnecessary. Instead, take a few moments to read and complete it (see figure 1.1).

Walking Health/Fitness Assessment

If you're going to walk, then you need an evaluation that will take activity and walking into consideration too. Figure 1.2 (on page 10) provides an assessment more specific to walking. It takes a look at your health history and your fitness background and level. In each of the 10 areas, choose the number that best describes you, then total the scores. The result tells you whether your baseline level is high, average, or low.

Walking Fitness Test

Now comes the real test, the one that will reveal the most about your walking fitness level because you will be doing just that—walking. Paper evaluations are one thing. This is the real deal.

Based partly on a test developed at The Cooper Institute in Dallas, Texas, the 1-mile walking test accurately evaluates general aerobic fitness levels for anyone 20 years old or older, of either gender and any body type (see figure 1.3 on page 13). Simply put, walk 1 mile as fast as you can and time yourself, then use the time to assess your walking fitness level.

Although not a precise laboratory test in which you're hooked up to gadgets and tubes that results in an exact number to quantify your ability to use oxygen (called $\dot{V}O_2$max), this evaluation will give you an excellent idea of your aerobic fitness and how much walking you can do. It will also help you determine the structure of your walking program.

One thing that might limit you during the test is inefficient walking technique, which is covered in chapter 2. That's okay. Don't worry about finesse—just move as quickly as you comfortably can. Your results might put you on or near the cusp between levels, but that's okay. Later you'll learn how to determine which level is right for you.

This evaluation also gives you an idea of where your lactate threshold is. That's the point where your body can't provide oxygen fast enough to hard-working muscles. Without oxygen, your muscles aren't fueled quickly enough.

Physical Activity Readiness
Questionnaire - PAR-Q
(revised 2002)

PAR-Q & YOU

(A Questionnaire for People Aged 15 to 69)

Regular physical activity is fun and healthy, and increasingly more people are starting to become more active every day. Being more active is very safe for most people. However, some people should check with their doctor before they start becoming much more physically active.

If you are planning to become much more physically active than you are now, start by answering the seven questions in the box below. If you are between the ages of 15 and 69, the PAR-Q will tell you if you should check with your doctor before you start. If you are over 69 years of age, and you are not used to being very active, check with your doctor.

Common sense is your best guide when you answer these questions. Please read the questions carefully and answer each one honestly: check YES or NO.

YES	NO		
☐	☐	1.	Has your doctor ever said that you have a heart condition <u>and</u> that you should only do physical activity recommended by a doctor?
☐	☐	2.	Do you feel pain in your chest when you do physical activity?
☐	☐	3.	In the past month, have you had chest pain when you were not doing physical activity?
☐	☐	4.	Do you lose your balance because of dizziness or do you ever lose consciousness?
☐	☐	5.	Do you have a bone or joint problem (for example, back, knee or hip) that could be made worse by a change in your physical activity?
☐	☐	6.	Is your doctor currently prescribing drugs (for example, water pills) for your blood pressure or heart condition?
☐	☐	7.	Do you know of <u>any other reason</u> why you should not do physical activity?

If

you

answered

YES to one or more questions

Talk with your doctor by phone or in person BEFORE you start becoming much more physically active or BEFORE you have a fitness appraisal. Tell your doctor about the PAR-Q and which questions you answered YES.

- You may be able to do any activity you want — as long as you start slowly and build up gradually. Or, you may need to restrict your activities to those which are safe for you. Talk with your doctor about the kinds of activities you wish to participate in and follow his/her advice.
- Find out which community programs are safe and helpful for you.

NO to all questions

If you answered NO honestly to <u>all</u> PAR-Q questions, you can be reasonably sure that you can:
- start becoming much more physically active – begin slowly and build up gradually. This is the safest and easiest way to go.
- take part in a fitness appraisal – this is an excellent way to determine your basic fitness so that you can plan the best way for you to live actively. It is also highly recommended that you have your blood pressure evaluated. If your reading is over 144/94, talk with your doctor before you start becoming much more physically active.

DELAY BECOMING MUCH MORE ACTIVE:
- if you are not feeling well because of a temporary illness such as a cold or a fever – wait until you feel better; or
- if you are or may be pregnant – talk to your doctor before you start becoming more active.

PLEASE NOTE: If your health changes so that you then answer YES to any of the above questions, tell your fitness or health professional. Ask whether you should change your physical activity plan.

<u>Informed Use of the PAR-Q</u>: The Canadian Society for Exercise Physiology, Health Canada, and their agents assume no liability for persons who undertake physical activity, and if in doubt after completing this questionnaire, consult your doctor prior to physical activity.

No changes permitted. You are encouraged to photocopy the PAR-Q but only if you use the entire form.

NOTE: If the PAR-Q is being given to a person before he or she participates in a physical activity program or a fitness appraisal, this section may be used for legal or administrative purposes.

"I have read, understood and completed this questionnaire. Any questions I had were answered to my full satisfaction."

NAME _____

SIGNATURE _____ DATE _____

SIGNATURE OF PARENT _____ WITNESS _____
or GUARDIAN (for participants under the age of majority)

Note: This physical activity clearance is valid for a maximum of 12 months from the date it is completed and becomes invalid if your condition changes so that you would answer YES to any of the seven questions.

 © Canadian Society for Exercise Physiology

Supported by: Health Santé
Canada Canada

continued on other side...

Figure 1.1 The Physical Activity Readiness Questionnaire.
Source: Physical Activity Readiness Questionnaire (PAR-Q) © 2002. Reprinted with permission from the Canadian Society for Exercise Physiology.

8

...continued from other side

PAR-Q & YOU

Physical Activity Readiness
Questionnaire - PAR-Q
(revised 2002)

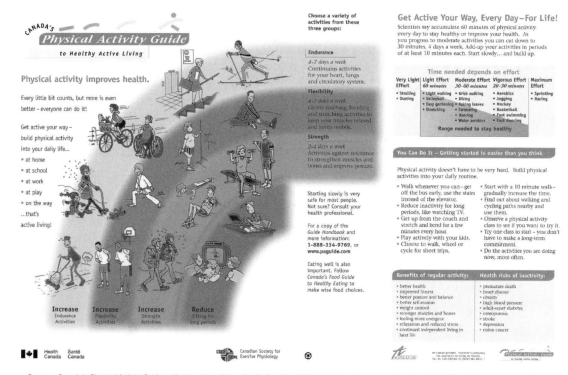

Physical activity improves health.

Every little bit counts, but more is even better – everyone can do it!

Get active your way –
build physical activity
into your daily life...

* at home
* at school
* at work
* at play
* on the way
...that's active living!

Choose a variety of activities from these three groups:

Endurance
4-7 days a week
Continuous activities for your heart, lungs and circulatory system.

Flexibility
4-7 days a week
Gentle reaching, bending and stretching activities to keep your muscles relaxed and joints mobile.

Strength
2-4 days a week
Activities against resistance to strengthen muscles and bones and improve posture.

Starting slowly is very safe for most people. Not sure? Consult your health professional.

For a copy of the *Guide Handbook* and more information:
1-888-334-9769, or
www.paguide.com

Eating well is also important. Follow *Canada's Food Guide to Healthy Eating* to make wise food choices.

Increase Endurance Activities
Increase Flexibility Activities
Increase Strength Activities
Reduce Sitting for long periods

Get Active Your Way, Every Day – For Life!

Scientists say accumulate 60 minutes of physical activity every day to stay healthy or improve your health. As you progress to moderate activities you can cut down to 30 minutes, 4 days a week. Add-up your activities in periods of at least 10 minutes each. Start slowly... and build up.

Time needed depends on effort

Very Light Effort	Light Effort 60 minutes	Moderate Effort 30-60 minutes	Vigorous Effort 20-30 minutes	Maximum Effort
• Strolling • Dusting	• Light walking • Volleyball • Easy gardening • Stretching	• Brisk walking • Biking • Raking leaves • Swimming • Dancing • Water aerobics	• Aerobics • Jogging • Hockey • Basketball • Fast swimming • Fast dancing	• Sprinting • Racing
	Range needed to stay healthy			

You Can Do It – Getting started is easier than you think

Physical activity doesn't have to be very hard. Build physical activities into your daily routine.

* Walk whenever you can – get off the bus early, use the stairs instead of the elevator.
* Reduce inactivity for long periods, like watching TV.
* Get up from the couch and stretch and bend for a few minutes every hour.
* Play actively with your kids.
* Choose to walk, wheel or cycle for short trips.

* Start with a 10 minute walk – gradually increase the time.
* Find out about walking and cycling paths nearby and use them.
* Observe a physical activity class to see if you want to try it.
* Try one class to start – you don't have to make a long-term commitment.
* Do the activities you are doing now, more often.

Benefits of regular activity:	Health risks of inactivity:
• better health • improved fitness • better posture and balance • better self-esteem • weight control • stronger muscles and bones • feeling more energetic • relaxation and reduced stress • continued independent living in later life	• premature death • heart disease • obesity • high blood pressure • adult-onset diabetes • osteoporosis • stroke • depression • colon cancer

Health Canada / Santé Canada

Canadian Society for Exercise Physiology

Source: *Canada's Physical Activity Guide to Healthy Active Living*, Health Canada, 1998 http://www.hc-sc.gc.ca/hppb/paguide/pdf/guideEng.pdf
© Reproduced with permission from the Minister of Public Works and Government Services Canada, 2002.

FITNESS AND HEALTH PROFESSIONALS MAY BE INTERESTED IN THE INFORMATION BELOW:

The following companion forms are available for doctors' use by contacting the Canadian Society for Exercise Physiology (address below):

The **Physical Activity Readiness Medical Examination (PARmed-X)** – to be used by doctors with people who answer YES to one or more questions on the PAR-Q.

The **Physical Activity Readiness Medical Examination for Pregnancy (PARmed-X for Pregnancy)** – to be used by doctors with pregnant patients who wish to become more active.

References:
Arraix, G.A., Wigle, D.T., Mao, Y. (1992). Risk Assessment of Physical Activity and Physical Fitness in the Canada Health Survey Follow-Up Study. **J. Clin. Epidemiol.** 45:4 419-428.
Mottola, M., Wolfe, L.A. (1994). Active Living and Pregnancy, In: A. Quinney, L. Gauvin, T. Wall (eds.), **Toward Active Living: Proceedings of the International Conference on Physical Activity, Fitness and Health**. Champaign, IL: Human Kinetics.
PAR-Q Validation Report, British Columbia Ministry of Health, 1978.
Thomas, S., Reading, J., Shephard, R.J. (1992). Revision of the Physical Activity Readiness Questionnaire (PAR-Q). **Can. J. Spt. Sci.** 17:4 338-345.

To order multiple printed copies of the PAR-Q, please contact the:

Canadian Society for Exercise Physiology
202-185 Somerset Street West
Ottawa, ON K2P 0J2
Tel. 1-877-651-3755 • FAX (613) 234-3565
Online: www.csep.ca

The original PAR-Q was developed by the British Columbia Ministry of Health. It has been revised by an Expert Advisory Committee of the Canadian Society for Exercise Physiology chaired by Dr. N. Gledhill (2002).

Disponible en français sous le titre «Questionnaire sur l'aptitude à l'activité physique - Q-AAP (revisé 2002)».

© Canadian Society for Exercise Physiology

Supported by: Health Canada / Santé Canada

Figure 1.1 *(continued)*

Walking Health/Fitness Assessment

Cardiovascular Health

Which of these statements best describes your cardiovascular condition? This is a critical safety check before you enter vigorous activity.

Warning: If you have a cardiovascular disease history, start the walking programs in this book only after receiving clearance from your doctor, and then only with close supervision by a fitness instructor.

No history of heart or circulatory problems _____ (3)

Past ailments treated successfully _____ (2)

Such problems exist, but no treatment is required _____ (1)

Under medical care for cardiovascular illness _____ (0)

Injuries

Which of these statements best describes your current injuries? This is a test of your musculoskeletal readiness to start a walking program.

Warning: If your injury is temporary, wait until it has healed before starting the program. If it is chronic, adjust the program to fit your limitations.

No current injury problems _____ (3)

Some pain in activity, but not limited by it _____ (2)

Level of activity limited by the injury _____(1)

Unable to do much strenuous training _____ (0)

Illness

Which of these statements best describes your current illness? Certain temporary or chronic conditions will delay or disrupt your walking program.

No current illness problems _____ (3)

Some problem in activity, but not limited by it _____ (2)

Level of activity limited by the illness _____ (1)

Unable to do much strenuous training _____ (0)

Age

In which of these age groups do you fall? Generally, the younger you are, the less time you have spent slipping out of shape.

Age 20 or younger _____ (3)

Age 21 to 29 _____ (2)

Age 30 to 39 _____ (1)

Age 40 and older _____ (0)

Figure 1.2   Walking Health/Fitness Assessment.

Weight

Which of these ranges best describes how close you are to your own definition of ideal weight? Excess fat, which can be layered on thin people too, is a sign of unhealthy inactivity. Of course, being underweight isn't ideal either. Be honest.

Within 3 pounds of your own ideal weight _____ (3)

Less than 10 pounds above or below your ideal weight _____ (2)

11 to 19 pounds above or below your ideal weight _____ (1)

20 or more pounds above or below your ideal weight _____ (0)

Resting Pulse Rate

Which of these ranges describes your current resting pulse rate, your pulse upon waking in the morning before getting out of bed? The heart of a fit person normally beats more slowly and efficiently than an unfit heart.

Below 60 beats per minute _____ (3)

61 to 69 beats per minute _____ (2)

70 to 79 beats per minute _____ (1)

80 or more beats per minute _____ (0)

Smoking

Which of these statements describes your smoking history and current habits? Smoking is the major demon behind ill health that can be controlled.

Never a smoker _____ (3)

Once a smoker, but quit _____ (2)

An occasional, social smoker now _____ (1)

A regular, heavy smoker now _____ (0)

Most Recent Walk

Which of these statements best describes your walking within the last month? Your recent participation in a specific activity best predicts how you will do in the future.

Walked nonstop for more than 1 brisk mile _____ (3)

Walked nonstop for 1/2 mile to 1 mile _____ (2)

Walked less than 1/2 mile and took rests _____ (1)

No recent walking of any distance _____ (0)

Figure 1.2 *(continued)*

(continued)

(continued)

Walking Background

Which of these statements best describes your walking history? Although fitness doesn't stick if you don't keep at it, if you once participated in an activity, you'll pick it up again more quickly.

Walked regularly within the last year _____ (3)

Walked regularly one to two years ago _____ (2)

Walked regularly more than two years ago _____ (1)

Never walked regularly _____ (0)

Related Activities

Which of these statements best describes your participation in other aerobic activities? Continuous activities such as running, cross-country skiing, and bicycling help build a good foundation for other similar activities, such as walking. Nonaerobic activities, such as weightlifting and stop-and-go sports like tennis, don't contribute as much to the base conditioning needed.

Regularly practice continuous aerobic activity _____ (3)

Sometimes practice continuous aerobic activity _____ (2)

Practice nonaerobic or stop-and-go sports _____ (1)

Not regularly active _____ (0)

TOTAL SCORE _____

Evaluate Your Score

≥ 20 points. You're high in overall health and fitness for a beginning walker. You could probably already handle 3- to 4-mile walks at a steady clip, four or five days a week.

10-19 points. Your rating is average, which is a fine place to be. You could start by walking fewer days, perhaps no more than three a week, and could cover a maximum of 2 to 3 miles each time.

< 10 points. Your score is low. You probably should start walking very short distances, for example, around the block a few times. Feel free to take plenty of breaks, building to $1\frac{1}{2}$ to 2 miles of easy walking that you can comfortably complete before you try a more challenging program.

Figure 1.2 *(continued)*

1-Mile Walking Test

For safety, make sure someone is with you when you complete this evaluation.

1. For an exact distance, use a track or a measured and marked flat trail with a smooth surface. A standard track is $\frac{1}{4}$ mile, so you will walk four laps in the inside lane for the 1-mile evaluation. Otherwise, use a measured path, a street you have measured with the odometer on your car, or a treadmill, all of which may be less accurate but close enough.

2. Warm up for several minutes with easy walking until your body feels warmer, then stretch.

3. Get ready to start your mile walk. Tips: Try to walk a pace that's steady but feels as if you're pushing hard. Remember, you'll probably walk at least 11 to 14 minutes, so don't start too fast. Pick up the pace in the last couple of minutes or last lap if you feel strong, which you should if you don't start too fast.

4. Your goal is to feel tired but not exhausted. You should feel slightly winded, but you should not gasp and pant.

5. Cool down by continuing to walk slowly for a few minutes after you are done.

6. Compare your time to the chart to assess your classification.

Minutes		Walking program
Men	Women	classification
<13:00	<14:00	Athletic
13:00-16:00	14:00-17:00	Fitness
>16:00	>17:00	Health

Figure 1.3 1-Mile Walking Test.

Your brain hits the panic button, and that dumps waste products such as lactic acid into your system, which causes the burning, heavy, exhausted sensation in your body that forces you to slow or stop. As you train harder, the threshold moves higher, meaning you'll be able to go faster longer before your body starts producing lactic acid. If you aren't limited by technique at your top speed, you may find your legs starting to feel heavy, and that feeling is one unscientific indication that you are nearing your threshold.

The faster you covered 1 mile, the higher your walking fitness level is. I specify *walking* fitness, because if you already exercise but you don't walk, you'll feel muscles after the test that you've never felt before. Even if you do walk but aren't used to pushing yourself for speed, you'll notice new muscles complaining.

Your 1-mile time places you in one of three walking program classifications. No matter which classification the test says you are, you can congratulate yourself for finishing. A low score only means that you have lots of room for improvement, which you'll see very quickly as you start training. Plan to repeat the test occasionally to check your progress and measure whether you should change your workouts to accommodate improving walking fitness.

Taking the walk test is important because it helps you decide with realistic data where you should start with the workouts in part II. Starting too low won't give you satisfactory gains, and starting too high will only frustrate you.

No matter where you start, learning to walk smoothly and more efficiently will help make your first steps fun and motivating. Seeing a skilled walker in action is like watching a great dancer. The flow is remarkable. The next chapter focuses on learning to feel that flow.

CHAPTER 2

Walking Technique

Put simply, walking is a series of forward falls. Keep falling forward, one foot after the other (without falling on your face, of course), and you'll move along in a straight line. Simple. Learned to do it as a toddler. Do it every day. So what's with this treatise on technique?

You're not walking just for transportation; you have goals. And technique will help you reach them. Technique becomes vital the more efficiently you want to move, the more quickly you want to go, the more you want to get fit by increasing intensity, *and* the more you want to avoid strains and pains.

Turning walking into a fitness activity demands a new dimension. Taking stock of how you move and smoothing that movement with the technique tips that follow turns your daily stride into a powerful, fitness-producing, calorie-burning strut. You may even be tempted to apply it to your strolls up and down the grocery aisles. However, this is only a primer on technique. If you are tantalized by these tips, you may want to refer to my other book, *Walking Fast,* which takes 40 pages to present walking technique. For most, though, this mini-lesson imparts enough know-how to get started, whether you walk for health or fitness, or as an athlete.

Before you start overanalyzing your fingers, toes, knees, and nose, let's get basic and think back to when you were little and your mom nagged you to stand up straight. She was right; no matter how fast or how far you go, standing tall is key. Hunching your shoulders tightens the chest and inhibits breathing. Dropping your chin to your chest does the same by closing off your throat. Instead, tighten your abdominal muscles, trying to bring them toward your back. Relax your shoulders and pull backward and then slightly downward with your shoulder blades. Avoid arching your back; this could strain your low back. One more thing: Keep breathing, please. Be careful though; walking should be simple. If you focus too intensely, you'll end up walking and looking like Frankenstein. Do the best you can, and if you don't get one point of technique, forget about it and try again later.

Bottom Half

Normally, the saying goes, "Take it from the top," but not when it comes to walking. Your bottom half is more important. So, maestro, let's take it from the bottom. Large major muscles in your lower body power you along. Take advantage of that strength, from hips to heels.

- **Heel to toe.** Compared to runners, who normally land more on the middle part of their feet—or even on their forefeet if moving faster or up or down hills—walkers should hit squarely on the heels with toes lifted high. That allows your ankle to move through its complete range of motion, from the heel landing in front of you at the beginning of the stride to the big toe pushing off behind you at the end of it. The toes and foot of the leg behind you at the end of the stride offer major propulsion as you pick up speed. Think about trying to leave your heel on the ground behind you a split second longer than normal, and feel as if you're trying to push the ground away from you with the ball of your foot before your foot leaves the ground to let the leg swing forward.

Here's a simple way to experience the correct motion: Sit in a chair and straighten your knee so that your foot is off the ground. Now flex your foot and lift the toes toward you (this is the heel plant part of the roll through), then slowly move your foot into a pointed position (this is the toe push-off part of the roll through). If you aren't used to this repetitive action while walking, you may feel a burning or tension in your shins. Don't worry. That's only an underused lower-leg muscle complaining, and it will get stronger as you walk more. You'll find tips on strengthening and stretching that area in chapter 5.

- **Stride.** Overstriding can turn your walk into a bouncing gallop reminiscent of Groucho Marx's comedy gait, which wastes energy that could be propelling you forward. Avoid the natural tendency to take longer strides to go faster, which is part of what runners do. Walkers, on the other hand, need to move their feet more quickly by taking more steps per minute—turnover, as it's called—while maintaining a natural stride length. Proper stride length prevents strains. Common complaints from overstriding include pain in the arch, knee, hip, and heel.

When walking at a slower pace of 17 or 18 minutes per mile, you might take 115 to 120 steps per minute, while a typical brisk walk at 15-minute-mile pace might generate 135 steps per minute. A speedy 12-minute mile might mean 160 steps per minute. The number of times you turn over your feet per minute increases as your walking speed increases. This means you'll feel smooth, like you're gliding. On the other hand, don't overexaggerate and turn your stride into short, choppy steps that diminish your natural power.

- **Hips.** Feel as if your leg starts at your waist. With each step, extend the leg slightly from above the hip bone. That frees your pelvis to rotate forward with each leg so you can cover more ground without bouncing. Avoid excessive side-to-side motion, which keeps your center of gravity from moving forward, which is of course the direction you want to go. Swinging the hips side to side also wastes energy; you want your energy to travel forward. Just relax in your hips and low back and let your body do what comes naturally. Tightening in your hips and back can also create back strain.

Top Half

Now that you understand the technique for your bottom half, it's time to move to the top. Your posture should be tall and erect no matter what your walking speed or level. Keep your chin tucked in, your ears over your shoulders, your eyes cast about 10 feet in front of you, your shoulders relaxed and pulled back, and your abdominals tightened. Dropping your chin or letting it protrude could produce tightness and strain in the back of your neck and upper back. Proper technique for your top half is important at any pace, but becomes even more so as you move faster.

- **Elbow bend.** Are you a bit intimidated or embarrassed by the idea of bending your elbows in right angles and pumping away like those way-too-serious-looking walkers you see on the streets? Don't be. This arm position serves two useful purposes. First, as you try to increase speed you'll find you can't swing the long lever of an extended arm as quickly as you can a shorter lever. And it feels awkward and may actually hurt to pump your arms while they're straight. Straight arms will keep you from achieving your speed potential. Who wants to be limited by an arm for goodness sake? Second, if your hands swell, bending your elbows helps keep blood and fluids from being pulled into your hands by gravity.

- **Arm swing.** Whether your arms are straight or bent, the pendulum action should happen at your shoulder. If you use a bent arm, the angle of your elbow joint shouldn't change during the swing. This puts extra strain on the ligaments and muscles and, again, wastes energy.

Also, control the bent-arm swing. It should be strong but remain close to your body. During the front portion of the movement, swing the hands no higher than the chest, tuck the elbows in at the waist, and don't allow the fingertips to cross the midline of your body or reach in front of you more than 10 to 12 inches. At the back portion of the movement, the elbow remains in its bent position. Power your arm swing with your back muscles, not your small shoulder-joint muscles. An added bonus is that the more you engage the back muscles in the arm swing, the more you'll tone them. Try to swing your arms faster, and your legs will likely mimic the speed.

• **Hands.** There's no need to clench your fist, unless you have a walking companion you want to punch out! Imagine you're holding a fragile raw egg in each cupped palm. Squeeze too hard and you'll break it; open too far and you'll drop it. Clenching can also cause pain in the forearm and wrist.

Technique Summary

Use this cheat sheet to remind yourself of the key points in good walking technique:

1. Stand tall, with your shoulders back and chest open.
2. As you step forward, lift your toes and plant the heel of your lead foot.
3. Roll through the entire foot and push off with your toes, lifting your heel high.
4. Avoid overstriding and bouncing.
5. Bend your elbows in a right angle so you can swing your arms faster.
6. Swing your arms from the shoulder and keep your elbows close to your sides.
7. Avoid clenching your hands.

Adjustments for Various Terrains

What I've discussed so far applies to any kind of terrain, but you'll experience different challenges when you head off road onto trails, grass, or sand. Depending on the softness of the surface or the hilliness of the terrain, you could use from a third more to double the amount of energy you would walking on smooth, paved surfaces. That can be an advantage. But if you're a beginner, you might tire more quickly, so take your off-road walks in short doses to start.

A few tips for walking on a different terrain start with focusing on your abdominal muscles. Keep them tight to support your back and add power to your stride. Tight abs also help keep you balanced and upright on loose or uneven surfaces. They are the key to just about every movement.

If you are on a trail with rocks, roots, or an otherwise uneven surface, try to step *between* obstacles to avoid slipping off them or twisting an ankle. Also, try to stay nimble. Rather than committing to each foot plant by landing solidly with all your weight on a flat foot, stay on your toes slightly so that if you start to slip or twist, you'll able to make the transition to the next foot quickly without disastrous results.

Hills demand different technique depending on if you're going up or down. On an uphill, use your toes and lower-leg muscles to push you forward *and up*. Use your arm swing as a mini-motor for extra power. And don't lean into the hill; this may strain your back (see "common walking errors" listed later).

On a downhill, what you do depends on how steep the hill is. On a minor to moderate downhill, soften or relax your knees just a bit to counteract the additional impact as gravity tries to pull each foot quickly to the ground. Rather than leaning back, remain upright. On a steeper downhill, you might be more comfortable zigzagging like a skier to lessen the steepness. You might also want to lean back *just a little* if the surface

Good posture will help you walk faster and prevent unnecessary strain.

is smooth and paved. If the surface of the hill is uneven or loose, don't sit back on your heels. This may throw your weight back, causing your feet to slip out from under you, leaving you on your behind.

Extra Demands of Race Walking

You don't have to *race* to race walk. But if you do compete in judged races, two rules apply: The knee of the supporting leg must straighten for a split second as it passes under the body, and the front heel must contact the ground before the rear foot leaves the ground. Although sometimes controversial (just like line calls in tennis or football), both are still judged by the human eye as of this writing.

Race walking has been around for centuries. Men's race walking became part of the Olympic Games in 1908, with competitors today testing their skills in 20- and 50-kilometer events, reaching average speeds of 6- to 7-minute miles for the distance. Women joined the Olympics in 1992 with a 10-kilometer race, in which many of them averaged 7-minute miles. The women's event was changed to 20 kilometers in the late 1990s, with many still approaching an average 7-minute-mile pace.

Race walking uses the basic, strong walking technique I've described, but it takes it a step further. The rear-toe push-off becomes almighty. Fast turnover distinguishes the champions from runners-up. Arm swings using the large back muscles power racers forward. Hip action, though, is what sets race walkers apart. Take a closer look at a good walker. The hip roll is simply a strong fitness walker's hip movement (as previously described), greatly exaggerated. Contrary to popular belief, it is not a side-to-side sashay. Any movement side to side detracts from the energy needed to push forward. The hip movement allows a walker to cover more ground per stride without bouncing, and the more ground a walker covers with each step, the more quickly he or she reaches the finish line. Good race walkers should look as if they're skimming the ground, nearly floating over its surface. Their heads should not change planes. Knees, as the rules state, must straighten upon heel landing. Note the word is straighten, not lock. Locking the knees can harm cushioning cartilage.

Studies have shown that the biomechanical breakpoint between walking and running—that point at which your body wants to run slowly because bounding off the ground actually takes less effort than walking fast—is a little slower than a 12-minute mile, or 4.8 to 4.9 miles per hour. What that means is that most people's bodies will naturally tell them to start running when they near that speed; if you've never tried to walk fast, you'll get a funny sensation as you near that point—as if someone were whispering in your ear, "Go ahead, run!" You actually have to use more muscle to continue to walk at that speed than if you indeed broke into a trot. This is where you will discover that indeed walking is not just slow running. Using more muscle means you also use more calories, and that's likely part of your goal with an activity program.

Correcting Common Walking Errors

Everybody moves differently, but walkers of all levels, from strollers to racers, make three common mistakes. Guard against them, because they inhibit your style and cause injuries.

1. Waist lean. If you have an ache in your low back after a walk, you may be tilting forward and letting your buttocks stick out. Not exactly attractive, let alone efficient or fitness inducing. Stand with your back against a wall. Now, tighten your abdominal muscles and lean forward only slightly from your ankles. That's the proper forward lean. Now lean forward, leaving your buttocks against the wall—that's the lean from the waist you want to avoid.

2. Overstriding. Does your hair, hat, or scarf flop up and down when you walk? That may be an indication that you are bouncing as you walk because you are overstriding. Slightly shortening your stride will usually eliminate the bounce and let you skim the ground. Every time your heel hits the ground in a stride that's too long, you're breaking your forward motion and forcing your body to move up and over into the next step, causing the bounce-along stride. Experiment with different stride lengths. Try a really long one, then a teeny, short one, then somewhere in between. Then find the equilibrium where you don't bounce.

3. Elbow whipping. The arm swing comes from the shoulder, not the elbow. Imagine punching something in front of you with one hand after the other as they alternatively swing forward. If you're actually "beating a drum" with up and down motions that come from your elbow bending and unbending, then you're doing it wrong. Try this experiment: Put a long piece of string around your neck and hold an end in each hand, making sure your elbows are bent at 90 degrees. Now walk. If you feel the string sliding back and forth behind your neck, that means you're beating the drum, pulling the string down to the right, then down to the left. Eliminating the string burn will eliminate the elbow whipping.

Safety Considerations and Etiquette

Walking for fitness is a cheater's way of sightseeing. You can tour places from your own city's neighborhoods to streets and villas in distant countries. Sure, paved trails and tracks can be a nice retreat, but they're unnecessary unless you're doing an advanced workout requiring timed paces and specific distances. Otherwise, anywhere that's safe is a walker's paradise. *Safe* is the operative word here. Once mindful of safety, think of your walks while you're traveling as an exploratory treat, not an exercise chore. The same applies to walks at home. Find a neighborhood or park you don't know and go for a visit.

No matter what, though, safety comes first, and etiquette for others isn't far behind. Follow these guidelines to stay safe, to share the road and track, and to always return unharmed:

1. If you can't use bike paths or sidewalks, walk on a road facing oncoming traffic. However, always walk on the outside of a blind curve.
2. Walk defensively. Don't assume the pedestrian right-of-way or challenge vehicles. Not every locale recognizes a pedestrian right-of-way.
3. Wear light-colored or reflective clothing as well as blinking safety lights at dusk, dawn, and night. Bright colors attract attention too. Or find tracks or other areas that are lit well at night.
4. Always carry identification with you in case of an accident or medical emergency. If you're traveling, carry the name of the hotel where you're staying and the name of an emergency contact at home or work.

5. If possible, walk with a companion. Otherwise, tell someone where you're going and when you expect to return. If you walk with your dog, he may increase safety, but make sure he's well trained and scoop his waste.

6. On a path, stay to the right so that faster walkers, runners, and cyclists or skaters can pass. Avoid pack walking—spreading your group across the entire trail—which clogs the way for others.

7. On a track, stay in the outside lanes, unless you're doing a structured, timed workout.

8. Leave the earphones and personal stereos at home so you'll be alert to dangers, be they animal, human, or urban.

Graceful, ground-skimming, invigorating walking requires focus on technique, but the right shoes and clothes can also contribute to an effective and enjoyable workout, especially when it's hot, cold, wet, or windy. In the next chapter, I tell you how to select appropriate apparel, shoes, and gear.

CHAPTER 3

Apparel and Gear

Walking's abundance of freedom and pleasure lies in its deficiency—a deficiency in required equipment, clothing, and accessories. Every time I head out for a walk on an area trail, I watch the bicyclists and in-line skaters prepare themselves. They unload equipment, adjust gears and wheels, strap themselves in, buckle up, pull on helmets, and pack up and slip on other gear. Although cycling and skating are certainly great and healthful activities—and ones I also participate in—the preparation on a day-to-day basis seems like an ordeal. Me, I just lace up my shoes, make sure I have on the right jacket or hat, and hit the trail or sidewalk. Now that's freedom!

The key item in every walker's closet is a well-fitting pair of supportive shoes. Because shoes are all you really need to embark on your walking program, it's important to know how to choose and take care of them, plus how to know when to replace them. There are other types of apparel and gear that walkers might find well suited for their needs, as well as extras that you might decide you want for the added motivation—or toy factor. You might decide to invest in a few pieces of apparel or various accessories as you get more involved. You must also consider fuel and fluids—not to be forgotten even if this is "just" walking because you still sweat and expend energy. Once outfitted, you'll be ready to head off to your free health club—your area parks, neighborhoods, and malls.

Importance of Good Walking Shoes

In walking you don't dress from head to toe, you dress from toe to head. Think of it this way: The snazziest, most finely tuned sports car on the road won't perform as it should without a solid set of appropriate, high-performance tires. Your body, too, won't be able to reach its full walking potential without a great pair of high-performance shoes. You see, walking isn't just slow running. Biomechanically, the body moves differently when it walks than when it runs, placing stresses in different places, in different ways, and at various degrees. Your body even moves slightly differently when you walk quickly compared to when you walk slowly. Simply put, walkers require a walking shoe. Brisk and athletic walkers require an athletic walking shoe.

Look for the following qualities in a walking-specific shoe:

- **Good heel cushioning**. Walkers strike the ground hardest on the heel rather than on the middle or front part of the foot, as most runners do. This heel strike leaves you for a nanosecond in a slightly precarious tippy position balanced on your heel, therefore demanding more heel stability in a shoe.

- **Flexible forefoot.** A walker's forefoot flexes at nearly twice the angle of a runner's at toe push-off, which requires more flexibility in the front of the shoe.

- **Roomy toe box.** The powerful push-off causes the toes to spread significantly, and the heel plant may cause the toes to lift more into the angle. These actions require a roomy, tall, and wide toe box, or front of the shoe.

- **Supportive heel construction and a low profile.** The higher, sometimes slightly flared heel typical of running shoes makes a walker less stable and acts as a fulcrum, causing the foot to slap down harder. That overworks the shin muscles, which can produce shin and ankle pain. A shoe with a lower profile, or lower heel, is more appropriate for walking.

- **Minimal underfoot cushioning and lateral support.** When walking, the impact on landing is about a third (or less) that of running. Walkers also only move in a linear, forward motion, so the emphasis on lateral support in shoes for racket sports, aerobics, or trail running is not useful.

Faster walkers, as well as those living in hotter climates or simply predisposed to hot feet, benefit from breathable mesh uppers so that a hot foot can cool quickly and sweat can evaporate during and after a walk.

You can easily drop as much as $120 on a high-end pair of walking shoes, but you can also get a good pair for $50 or $60. Any cheaper than that (unless it's a great closeout deal) and the shoe probably only looks the part and will break down or cause injury. Some fitness and general interest magazines publish annual surveys of walking shoes, but don't take a rating as gospel because you never know if the advertising department influenced the outcome. You might get recommendations from a friend or colleague too, but your movement, support, and cushioning needs may be different. Over the last several decades, the number of and variety in walking shoes have increased greatly, but that also means you may become utterly baffled by the choices.

Start your search for the perfect walking shoe on the Internet. Go to major shoe manufacturers' Web sites and read about their shoes. This will help you pare your long list to a few based on those descriptions. If you stumble across a shoe review on an unknown site, question it and the source. It might be legit, but you don't know that (anybody can slap something up on the Web and call himself or herself an expert).

Next, go to a specialty athletic footwear store and try on all the name brands, even those you may have picked out on the Web sites you visited. A good store will let you take a quick jaunt down the sidewalk or hall, and its staff will even watch you move to see if the shoe is right for you. I am not against large sporting goods stores, but in some cases you receive less help, less-informed help, and sometimes even old models. Be warned, if you have made it clear you're a walker, do *not* listen to or buy from a sales person who tells you that you should buy a running shoe. Go to a different store. The sales clerk is either uninformed or a running snob. (Exception: If you plan to walk *and* run, you are better off with a flexible, low-profile running shoe so that you also get enough cushioning for that higher-impact activity of running.)

If you still haven't found what you want or a specific shoe you saw on the Web, ask about special orders. Many stores will do this and might not even require a deposit or a guarantee you'll buy (be sure to ask so that you aren't surprised). You can also contact the manufacturer directly if you can't find the model you liked or the size or width you need; manufacturers can often recommend you to retailers they work with or to online retailers who carry a full virtual warehouse with a broader selection. Some manufacturer Web sites include searchable directories of their retailers.

What about aesthetics? Walking shoes used to look like nursing shoes—all white, all leather or synthetic, and really boring and grandmotherly looking. No more! Today's walking shoes can have as much flash, style, and color as you want. Have fun with that.

If you plan to do many workouts on trails or hills with loose or uneven terrain or rocks, consider those needs. Look for better grip and stability and even a light hiker, or what some companies call brown walkers or country walkers—walking shoes that look a little like a hiking shoe. They are still lightweight, but usually come in darker colors. Features might include a higher top for ankle support (only good if you plan to do more hiking), deeper tread and stickier outsole for nonslip walking over dirt and rocks, better lateral stability, and a higher heel to ease Achilles tendon tension while you're walking uphill. Some may also be made of Gore-Tex or other waterproof or water-resistant materials for rainy or wet outings.

If you're interested in race walking, you need special shoes designed for the sport's high speeds that exaggerate basic walking technique. They have much flatter soles to better skim the ground and to accommodate the increased ankle flexion upon heel strike, plus they have slipperlike forefoot flexibility. There are a few race-walking shoes on the market, but many people end up in basic lightweight running shoes.

Your shoes might look great from the outside for years, but the insides lose about a third of their ability to support and absorb shock after 500 to 600 miles. For example, an average walker—someone putting in 3 miles three or four times a week—needs replacement shoes after about a year. Walk more and you need new ones more often.

Shoes should be able to go from store shelf to workout without a hitch. Still, a new pair of shoes might pinch in a different place or cause you to land differently than you're accustomed to. Just the fact that the materials in your new pair aren't broken down causes them to fit your feet differently. Try out new shoes on short or easy workouts to make sure they don't cause soreness, blisters, or strain.

Be continually aware of how your feet and body feel. More experienced walkers know a shoe is ready to trade in when they get a particular ache in the ankles or hips. Watch the tread to see where it's wearing out, and compare the soles of both shoes to each other. Are they permanently tilted one way or the other (perhaps one more than the other) when you put them on a table and look at them from behind? Does one foot have more wear than another? That test will give you an idea of where your gait may be uneven.

The wear pattern on the bottom of your worn-out shoes might be an indication of needless pain on the horizon. Shoes aren't the place to be chintzy. Retire the old ones to shopping trips or gardening, and keep your good walking shoes just for fitness walking so that they last longer.

Few people have perfect feet. Most either supinate (roll outward) or, more commonly, pronate (roll inward). High or low arches might also demand extra attention. If you are plagued by injury, a foot malfunction might be the problem. You may just need a different shoe, one with more support or cushioning. Drug- and sports stores sell a range of heel cushions, arch supports, and other inserts you can try. Podiatrists can also analyze and measure your feet for personal orthotics, if needed.

A few tips will help your investment last as long as possible:

- Don't put shoes by a heat source to dry because that will crack and weaken the materials.

- Remove the insoles after each walk so they can dry more easily. If you have two pairs (a good idea, by the way), alternate using them so that each can fully dry between wearings.

- If your shoes get particularly wet or sweaty, stuff them with wads of newspaper or bags of cedar shavings after working out. Both help shoes keep their shape and soak up moisture and salts from sweat that break down materials.

Choosing the Right Clothes

With good shoes on your feet, you're nearly ready to hit the road. Although great shoes are the key ingredient, carefully considered clothes will make your workouts more comfortable.

Next to shoes, socks are your best friend. Avoid cotton; synthetic fibers are better at drawing moisture away from your skin and they don't end up soggy. Wet socks rub and cause blisters, besides being uncomfortable. Consider some of the newer and finer wool socks; they've come a long way. Look for snugly fitting socks with as few seams to chafe as possible. For some blister-prone people, wearing two thin pairs of socks can eliminate rubbing. Consider trying on your socks of choice with your shoes when you shop because thicker socks may alter the fit you need.

Tops, whether short- or long-sleeved, should be comfortable and allow you to swing your arms freely. They can either be loose or snug, but avoid bulky seams. The best clothing is made of high-tech synthetic materials that breathe and wick moisture away from your skin, keeping you cooler in hot weather and warmer in cold. Although they can be more expensive than that old T-shirt in your drawer, I'd bet my bottom dollar that you will love any lightweight technical shirt you get that is made for activity and sweating. If you aren't prepared to invest the money, your next best bet is a natural fiber, such as cotton, especially for indoor workouts where the elements aren't a big factor.

Bottoms, from sweats to shorts, can be loose fitting without bulky seams between your thighs to irritate or chafe, or skin tight, depending on your personal comfort level. Long tights in the winter and thigh-length tights in the summer protect and support well. Here, too,

The right apparel and gear can make your workout safer and more comfortable, especially in the extremes of cold and warm weather conditions.

high-performance wicking fabrics are available, as are blends with Lycra. Personal preference and budget play the largest role in your decision.

Headgear is important to protect you from the sun in the summer and retain body heat in the winter. If you're worried about sun, consider a cap with a drape in the back to protect your neck or a hat with a wide brim. In the winter, cover up with wind- or waterproof shells and, if in a really cold climate, shell pants, preferably those that are breathable to allow your sweat to evaporate. Layers work best—not only to trap your body heat, but to peel off as you heat up or put on as you cool down. I can't begin to explain the choices in jackets, but I will tell you that the windbreaker has changed a lot. There are all levels of windproof, water-resistant, and waterproof jackets with hoods or not, with full or half zippers, with pockets or not, or with underarm zippers or not. Check out local specialty running stores (they carry lightweight outerwear good for walking or running), sporting goods stores, or even an outdoor specialty store. Although outdoor specialty stores may cater to backpackers and hikers, the outerwear (as well as gloves and headgear) crosses over well. Hands, too, need protection in the cold. For cool days, lightweight glove liners are fine. Otherwise look for thermal mittens or gloves or those made of moisture-wicking materials. All those technical fibers, including those that repel water or stop wind, are also available in gloves and mittens. Consider these items an investment in your comfort. If you're comfortable, you'll be much more likely to keep up your walking program.

Preparing for the Climate

Weather variations make any outdoor activity, including walking, more complicated and layers more important. Of course, it's also the weather that makes being outdoors a lot more enjoyable too, as long as you correctly layer the right protective gear and apparel. In cold weather, try to pick a warmer part of the day for your workout and the warmest days for your harder walks. Cover your ears, nose, and fingertips; these parts of your body are most susceptible to frostbite. If you're particularly susceptible to the cold, carry extra sweats or an oxygen-activated heat pack for after your workout (these are little carbon-filled bags that, when opened, become cozy hand warmers that produce heat for about eight hours). Remove sweaty, wet clothing as soon as possible after your workout because the moisture will continue to draw heat from your cooling body. Be aware of the early signs of frostbite (tingling, numbness, or burning in the extremities) or hypothermia (pallor, mental confusion, or cold extremities).

Hot climates are always a challenge, particularly because humidity can make a difference in effort and potential danger. Wear white clothing, which better reflects the hot sun. Even lightweight, loose, long-sleeved, white shirts can reflect heat better than bare arms. Try soaking a hat in cool water before wearing it, and punch holes in it so your body heat can escape. Drink plenty of water before and after your workout, and don't be afraid to sweat. Sweat acts as your body's natural evaporative air cooler. Stay alert for signs of heat exhaustion and heatstroke: weak or rapid pulse, headache, dizziness, weakness, lack of sweating, and hot and dry skin. Normally you need a week or two to get used to the heat. But that means you have to go out for easier walks, not sit on the porch sipping iced tea. Just take it easy when it first gets hot and avoid the hottest part of the day. You can also consider finding a mall or gym where you can walk indoors on extremely cold or hot days.

Heat–Humidity Readings

Keep the following hot-weather ratings table handy for reference on hot days (see table 3.1). Find the temperature on the left side of the scale and the relative humidity percentage on the top. Find where these two readings converge. A temperature below 75 degrees Fahrenheit is normally always safe ("A" ratings), and one above 95 degrees is almost always unsafe ("F" ratings), no matter what the humidity. Use good judgment when ratings fall from "B" to "D." The typical advice is to exercise outdoors during cooler morning hours, but that doesn't necessarily hold true in humid climates. When it's warmer, such as in the late evening in humid areas, the air has a higher moisture-holding capacity, so the same amount of moisture in the air will result in a lower overall relative humidity.

Table 3.1 Heat/Humidity Chart

	Humidity Level (Percent)								
Temperature	20	30	40	50	60	70	80	90	100
70°F/22°C	A	A	A	A	A	A	A	B	B
75°F/24°C	A	A	A	A	A	B	B	B	C
80°F/26°C	A	A	B	B	B	B	C	C	C
85°F/29°C	B	B	C	C	C	D	D	D	F
90°F/32°C	C	C	D	D	D	F	F	F	F
95°F/35°C	D	D	F	F	F	F	F	F	F

Reprinted, by permission, from R.L. Brown, 2003, *Fitness Running*, 2nd ed. (Champaign, IL: Human Kinetics), 38.

Wind-Chill Readings

Use the cold-weather ratings table for windy winter days (see table 3.2). Locate the day's wind speed on the left side of the scale and the temperature across the top. Find where these two readings converge. A temperature above 35 degrees Fahrenheit is normally always safe ("A" ratings), and one below 10 degrees below zero is almost always unsafe ("F" ratings), no matter what the wind speed. Again, use good judgment when ratings fall from "B" to "D."

Table 3.2   Cold-Weather Ratings

Wind Reading	Temperature									
Fahrenheit	35°	30°	25°	20°	15°	10°	5°	0°	−5°	−10°
Celsius	1°	−1°	−3°	−6°	−8°	−10°	−12°	−15°	−17°	−19°
Calm	A	A	A	B	B	B	C	C	C	D
5 mph (2 mps)	A	A	B	B	B	C	C	C	D	D
10 mph (5 mps)	A	B	B	B	C	C	C	D	D	D
15 mph (7 mps)	B	B	B	C	C	C	D	D	D	F
20 mph (9 mps)	B	B	C	C	C	D	D	D	F	F
25 mph (11 mps)	B	C	C	C	D	D	D	F	F	F
30 mph (13 mps)	C	C	C	D	D	D	F	F	F	F
35 mph (15 mps)	C	C	D	D	D	F	F	F	F	F
40 mph (17 mps)	C	D	D	D	F	F	F	F	F	F

Reprinted, by permission, from R.L. Brown, 2003, *Fitness Running*, 2nd ed. (Champaign, IL: Human Kinetics), 38.

Trinkets, Toys, and Other Accessories

Walking's beauty is certainly its simplicity, but a few extra items or tubes stuffed in a bag can make you more comfortable. Your budding interest might also heed the call of an array of other helpful gadgets.

• Strange as it may seem, petroleum jelly is probably a walker's best friend. Spread a little on your inner thighs, under your arms, or between an elastic underwear strap and skin to prevent painful chafing. You can also find other antirub products in sports stores.

• Sun protection is vital—always and without exception. Use one with a rating of 30 SPF. Men, don't forget the back of your neck. Women, don't forget the backs of your knees. Look for sunblock that is fragrance free and geared for use during sport and activities. Some companies make sprays, too, which are convenient for legs, backs, and (yes, men) tops of heads.

• Sunglasses reduce eyestrain and eye damage. They aren't just for looks, so invest in a good pair.

• A digital watch will help you time your workouts or just note the time of day so that you get home when you're supposed to. As you advance, you might consider a sports watch, with lap memory, so you can time segments and track your progress.

• High-tech heart rate monitors aren't exclusively for competitors, although they may be one of those toys you add to your walker's closet as you progress. You can get basic models for about $50 that show your heart rate and workout time. Fancy models with target zones, lap timing, memory, recovery time, and all kinds of other doodads can run $100, $200, and up. Whatever your fitness level, this gadget can accurately monitor your heart rate to help you stay safely where you belong for that day's workout. The most accurate are those with a band you wear around your chest to measure your heart rate from the source, compared to those that take your pulse from a fingertip.

• Pedometers have come of age in the last decade, going from mostly inaccurate to fairly well made. You can get basic models for $10 to $30. Of course, leave it to the tech wizards to take a good thing perhaps too far. There are now pedometers with timers, alarms, radios, and even heart rate monitors, and those are priced accordingly. If you use a pedometer to estimate your distance, be sure the stride length is set correctly and the terrain you're covering doesn't change much.

Wearing a pedometer can be a fun and motivating way to gauge your pace and distance.

• Personal stereos might be entertaining, but they can be dangerous. They can damage hearing and block traffic noise or even the sounds of approaching dogs and people. It's best to leave yours at home, but if you really can't do without, keep the volume low or listen with one ear only.

• The use of hand weights while running or walking has been debated by medical and exercise professionals for years. To make a long story short, dangling a pair from your fingers doesn't do much more than strain ligaments and muscles in your shoulders, elbows, and hands. Gripping a weight can cause high blood pressure, too. Muscle toning isn't increased, and the increased calorie usage is insignificant. Weighted vests are another matter. Although safer on joints in your arms and legs, they can make a basic fitness walk more difficult and exhausting. They are best reserved for the very advanced or someone training for an endeavor that involves carrying weight, such as backpacking or adventure racing.

Fuel and Fluids

Although many of you may be taking up a walking program to lose weight (and it is indeed effective with consistency), don't starve your body for energy or forget to hydrate properly. Food is energy. It fuels your exercise, and that keeps you putting one foot in front of the other. That said, you won't use more than about 50 to 100 calories per mile on a moderately brisk walk, so you don't want to overdo the intake. If you plan to go for a walk at the end of the day, however, and if you haven't eaten all day, you may end up feeling exhausted. Do yourself a favor and eat a small prewalk snack such as fruit, fresh or dried, or a few bites of a sports energy bar, or some other quality nibble. If you plan to head out for two hours or more, take a sports energy bar or fruit to keep you powered. Racers in different foot-powered activities may need up to 300 calories an hour at high intensities, but you'll need less, albeit still some.

When it comes to hydration, that's an entirely different story. Everybody needs water and fluids. During exercise, you need about 6 to 16 ounces of water an hour, assuming it's not particularly hot and you aren't working out at a very high intensity. Normally, if you are going for 2 to 3 miles, you should be fine drinking a glass of water before you leave and swigging more when you return. However, if it's extra humid or hot, err on the side of caution and carry water. If you plan to walk longer, always carry water. All kinds of water belts and packs are available, from those with reservoirs and drinking tubes to belts around your waist that hold bottles. Check out sporting goods, running specialty, or outdoor specialty stores to see which design best fits you and your needs.

What about sport drinks? Unless you're out for more than an hour, you have no need to take in the extra calories; stick with water. If you're going to walk longer or it's very hot or humid, sip on a sport drink that isn't too sweet and contains sodium and potassium.

Now that you have supportive shoes on your feet and appropriate clothing and other gear, it's time to get technical. Let's move on to training formulas, information about heart rate, stretching, and strengthening—information you'll need before you can set out to make great strides.

Training Guidelines

Pulling together the parts to a walking program shouldn't be complicated. That's one of the joys of walking and probably one of the reasons you've chosen walking as a key to becoming regularly active and healthier. It should be easier to make walking a part of your lifestyle than most other activities. Still, you should consider some guidelines for a safe and effective program whether you're young or old, competitive or moderate, or a former jock or a beginning fitness exerciser.

Planning Your Walking Program

Everyone should take time to contemplate something like an exercise and walking program before getting started. It's a big step that takes commitment, time, and learning how to tune in to your body. In fact, if addressed correctly, these preliminary steps can be instrumental in your success as you learn to make walking a part of your life each week.

Listening to Your Body

The human body is a smart machine; if only we'd pay attention to the subtle and not-so-subtle messages it sends us daily. The more you exercise, the more you'll find yourself in tune with those signals, and that's good. Listening to your body can make the difference between getting hurt and walking injury free, or getting sick and staying healthy. It can also translate into better awareness in your day-to-day life.

Listen to the little owies, pains, and twinges in your joints and muscles as soon as they start. If something aches for more than two or three days, you probably should consult a doctor. Bottom line, the sooner you pay attention to an ache or excessive fatigue, the lower the chance it will affect you long term or to a serious extent. Other signals are important too, because your ability to exercise fluctuates based on fatigue, stress, your previous workout, illness, your workload, emotions, and even the weather. All those can affect your body's engine—the heart. Learn to take your resting heart rate (before you get out of bed in the morning, see page 40 for instructions) and to note your pulse before, during, and after workouts. If your resting heart rate is 10 percent higher than normal, consider taking the day off or slipping in a very easy workout. If your pulse is higher than normal *before* a workout, take it easier; the elevated heart rate could be a result of fatigue, stress, or even an impending virus. If your pulse doesn't recover as quickly as usual afterward, plan a day off or an easy day the next day.

Taking It Easy

Eagerness will take you far, but doing too much can bring soreness, injury, and an early end to good intentions. If you are new to walking or new to exercise, it is easy to be so enthusiastic that you get sucked into doing too much. The most common mistake beginners at any kind of exercise make is too much, too soon, too fast, too hard, or some combination of those. Normally, the body (and mind) can and will hold out for four to eight weeks. Then something will give, and you'll be back at square one. So be smart and start slowly and easily.

Two rules apply:

1. The 10 percent rule. Increase your mileage by no more than about 10 percent from one week to the next. If you have to take time off (because of illness or for a vacation), start back at a lower level rather than where you left off and build again. Exception: Someone who is already a regular exerciser may increase from week to week by as much as 20 percent.

2. The hard–easy rule. Alternate every hard workout with rest or an easy workout to allow your muscles to recuperate and heal. A hard workout is either faster or longer than normal *for you*. For a beginner, a hard workout is any walk. For novices, the hard–easy rule means walking only every other day. If you're a moderate walker, either take a day off or do an easy workout after a hard one. And an advanced walker should rotate long or fast workouts with one or two days of easy ones. But that doesn't mean not taking a day off, especially as you get older.

Evaluating Your Schedule

For most of us, life's time constraints hamper what we'd like to do, what we know we should do, and what we really can do. So take a moment to evaluate your time using the chart in figure 4.1. This tool gives an amazingly realistic assessment of your life's demands. Go ahead and redo it as your schedule changes.

We all have 168 hours in a week. Nobody has any more or any less. Take a moment to log the time you spend on duties and requirements, from sleeping and commuting, to driving the kids to ballgames and taking showers. Then subtract each from the 168. Be sure to count 10 hours or so for those pesky general tasks such as stopping at the dry cleaners and the bank.

Do you have hours left for walking? Great—you'll have no problem reaching your personal potential. Or is your time account in the red before you even get to exercise? Look at how you allot your time and decide if you can steal an hour or so for exercise from another category. Do you find that you spend an extra 30 minutes in the evenings doing nothing you can put your finger on? Reassess these black holes of time and see what you can suck back out. Do you have a goal of walking six days a week for an hour but now see that you only have two free hours? You must decide where your priorities are and perhaps start with less walking time as you learn to juggle the demands in your schedule.

Try to get in at least three 20-minute walks a week. As you progress, you can aim for three to five weekly exercise sessions of 20 to 60 minutes (as recommended by the American College of Sports Medicine for quality cardiovascular improvement). But any activity, even going a few blocks with a friend, or taking the stairs instead of the elevator, can help improve your health.

Evaluating Your Time

Hours in a week		168
Sleeping	_____ per day × 7 =	–_____
Personal hygiene	_____ per day × 7 =	–_____
Eating	_____ per day × 7 =	–_____
Working/commuting	_____ per day × 7 =	–_____
Family commitments	_____ per day × 7 =	–_____
School/homework	_____ per day × 7 =	–_____
General tasks	_____ per day × 7 =	–_____
Shopping	_____ per day × 7 =	–_____
Recreation/relaxation	_____ per day × 7 =	–_____
Other	_____ per day × 7 =	–_____
Remaining hours for exercise		_____

Figure 4.1 Chart to use in time evaluation.

Choosing Your Walking Location

Another aspect of planning your walking program is determining where to walk. Remember that your schedule, available time, and type of workout planned play a role in where you head. Here are a few possibilities with descriptions of their advantages.

* **Treadmill.** The sample programs describe outdoor workouts. One of the joys of walking is getting out from inside four walls, but sometimes circumstances—weather, convenience, travel, kids that need watching—mean you'll want to stay inside on a treadmill. So with a simple conversion from minutes per mile to miles per hour (mph) you can also accomplish these workouts on a treadmill. See table 4.1 for that conversion.

Table 4.1	Converting Minutes per Mile to Miles per Hour
Min/mile	**Miles/hour**
25-30	2-2.4
21-24	2.5-2.9
18-20	3-3.3
16½-17½	3.4-3.6
15-16	3.8-4
13-14	4.3-4.6
12½-13	4.6-4.8
11½-12	5-5.2
<11	>5.5

There's nothing wrong with treadmill workouts. They can have benefits that outdoor walking doesn't provide. You can control exactly how far and how fast you go, and you can incorporate hills at a whim, as often or as steep as you want. Using a treadmill also lets you walk before or after dark when it might be unsafe outdoors. And you can even watch TV or otherwise distract yourself on those days when you don't much feel like walking. Plus, you can have water or a change of clothes handy, and you don't have to worry about the weather.

You'll find that increasing the incline to 3 to 5 percent won't make a huge difference in your perception of the workout's intensity. However, perception is the key word here. Once you reach about 7 or 8 percent, you will definitely feel as if you're going up. Use inclines of 10 percent or more sparingly because they are intense. If you decide to incorporate inclines to add intensity, choose one that allows you to remain comfortable while walking naturally, with your arms bent or hanging at your sides. If you have to hang onto the front rail to keep up with the speed (and end up looking like you're water-skiing), the incline is too steep. However, to more accurately equate your speed on a treadmill to speed in the open air, you need to add an approximately 1 percent incline. This 1 percent incline requires about the same amount of energy as the wind resistance you encounter when walking on the ground or a track but don't encounter on a treadmill.

- **Mall.** If you don't feel safe outside, you're bothered by the cold or heat, or you can't seem to get out after the sun rises or before it sets, call around to your local enclosed malls. Many open early for walkers. If you can't make it in the morning, an evening workout dodging dawdling shoppers is better than not working out at all. Another advantage of a mall workout are stairs (if it's a two-story building). Adding a stint up and down on each lap can increase your intensity and muscle strengthening.

- **City streets.** If you live in the heart of a city or are traveling to the city, you can get a great workout by taking advantage of the sites and other built-in features. Again, you can add a flight of stairs at the transit station or shops. Try to be flexible with your route so you don't have to stop at too many traffic lights; cross at the street that gives you the walk signal first. Do keep in mind that headphones are especially dangerous in busy cities, so it's best to leave them at home.

- **Tracks.** Another option is the local track, either dirt or a slightly cushioned surface called all-weather, which feels slightly rubberized. They can also be a super place to feel safe because others gather there after dark or before sunrise to get in laps and miles. Some are even lighted at night. Plus, if you want to get a better feel for your pace or distance covered, the exact quarter-mile distance can help. However, pay attention to the etiquette guidelines on track usage discussed in chapter 2, page 21. You must also pay attention to when the track is reserved for the school's team practices and avoid those times. However, I've used tracks during practices, with the permission of the coach of course, and just stuck to outside lanes.

- **Parks.** Many cities have parks with paths that circle and loop, or even linear parks and recreational paths that attract walkers, cyclists, and runners. Call your local park district to find out where these are and what the facilities include. They can be gems in a city, with paths that are well used and safe. But do inquire about safety because some sections may be little used and too isolated for safety. Remember, no headphones (or one ear only) because the music can block the sounds of ill-intentioned passersby or even of traffic.

- **Trails.** If you live in a city, there's no reason why you can't escape your urban area on the weekend and transform your walk into more of a hike, hitting the dirt trails and hills or forests nearby. Your technique will change a bit going up and down hills, and you may find yourself moving more slowly because softer surfaces require more energy. But no matter, it's a great escape. Just go by time and keep moving for an entirely different experience that can help you breathe fully without being pounded by city noises and traffic. You may like this so much, a weekend outing will become a permanent part of your schedule!

Don't feel as if you have to forsake your friends, family, children, or even your dog as you build your walking program. They can take part in your program and benefit from it as well. If you have a young child, check out the various sport or jogger strollers that have three wheels and a sturdy construction (some with rain and sun shields). Depending on the thickness of the tires and sturdiness of the chassis, these strollers can also perform well on dirt trails. If you have an older child, let him or her ride a bike along with you. Another idea is to start a "soccer parent" walking group. While your children are engrossed in their activity (soccer, swimming, track, etc.), the parents can use their time wisely by doing laps around the field or school.

If you own a dog, taking him along with you may help you feel safer, but be sure he has the proper training. If it's okay to let him off the leash, make sure he responds quickly to voice commands. If letting him off-leash is not permitted, there are specialty hands-free leashes available, which attach to your waist. You'll also need to bring bags for scooping up his waste, treats for good behavior, and a source of water.

Using Training Formulas and Charts

As you head out the door, you may want to determine how fast you're going, how far you're going, how many calories you're using, and if you're walking hard (or easy) enough. You should start a workout log so you can monitor your progress. Use the log on page 46 as a template.

Determining Your Pace

To decide what distances you can walk and at what speed, look back to the assessments in chapter 1. Your answers for the walking fitness assessment placed you in one of three groups: high, average, or low. Now cross-check that rating with your result in the walking health/fitness assessment, also in chapter 1, where you paced off a quick mile. Your time ranked you in one of three classifications, from high (athletic walking) to low (health walking).

A high rating in the first assessment will most likely correspond with a high rating in the walk, an average will match up with a moderate in the walk, and a low rating will match up with a low in the walk. If your results were this clear-cut, the following table shows you which walking program will be right for you (see table 4.2). But if the two didn't mesh so neatly, use your rating for the 1-mile walk to guide you into a walking program. Your mile time demonstrated what you can do when you're putting one foot in front of the other.

Remember, however, this is only a guide. If you find yourself on the border between levels, be conservative to start and follow the easier program. Gradually explore the more intense workouts until you find what's right for you for the long term. Feel free to mix and match workouts if you find yourself somewhere in the middle. That's the beauty of five categories of workouts with a wide range of levels—there will be workouts to match every variation in personal fitness levels and daily energy swings. Always listen to your body. A complete and accurate assessment also includes internal feedback. If your ranking places you in the athletic walker category, but you have no desire to move that fast, then move back to a more moderate program. The same goes for those ranked in the moderate level; step back to an easier program if that will fulfill your walking wishes and help you achieve your health goals.

Retake the 1-mile timed walk test every month or so to see how you're progressing and to gain the confidence to pump up your program.

Table 4.2 Choosing a Program

Walking health fitness assessment	1-mile walking test	Walking program
High	High	Athletic walking
Average	Moderate	Fitness walking
Low	Low	Health walking

Assessing Your Heart Rate

Over the years, formulas to assess appropriate workout heart rates have come under incredible scrutiny. Recent research investigates the accuracy of simplistic formulas such as the one that follows. The bottom line is, no mathematical formula will provide an exact workout heart rate. They are all estimates, at best, a starting point for getting to know your body and what feels good or not so good. I won't take sides in the heart rate battle but instead give you a couple of formulas. Plug your data into both to see how they compare.

Simple Formula

If you're a man, subtract your age from 220:

$$220 - \text{age} = \text{maximum heart rate (max HR)}$$

Then multiply your chosen goal or intensity by the result. For example, a 40-year-old man undertaking a moderate workout would follow this formula:

$$220 - 40 = 180 \text{ (max HR)} \times 70\% \text{ (lower end of moderate range)} = 126$$

$$180 \times 79\% \text{ (upper end of moderate range)} = 142$$

Therefore, his target heart rate range for moderate workouts is 126 to 142, with the exact target depending on the workout selected.

Women use a similar formula, substituting 226 for 220:

$$226 - \text{age} = \text{max HR}$$

Then multiply your chosen goal or intensity by the result. For example, a 30-year-old woman who intends to do a moderate workout would follow this equation:

$$226 - 30 = 196 \text{ (max HR)} \times 70\% \text{ (lower end of moderate range)} = 137$$

$$196 \times 79\% \text{ (upper end of moderate range)} = 155$$

This woman's target heart rate range for moderate workouts is 137 to 155, with the exact target depending on the workout selected.

Resting Heart Rate Formula

The formula using resting heart rate (RHR) is the same as the simple formula, except it subtracts your resting heart rate after you subtract your age and then adds it back in later. This of course only works if you *know* your resting heart rate. Guessing isn't good enough. Determine your resting heart rate by taking it before you get out of the bed in the morning—before you've been active or moving around much and before you've been jolted by the screech of an alarm clock. It can still be difficult to obtain, but give it a whirl. Highly trained athletes can have resting rates in the 30s and 40s! The rest of the population will be in the 50s to 70s, depending on condition, drugs that lower or raise heart rate, and disease.

If you're a man, subtract your age from 220 to get your max HR, then subtract your RHR:

$$220 - \text{age} = \text{max HR} - \text{RHR} = \text{max HR II}$$

So, for a 40-year-old man, the formula would work like this:

$$220 - 40 = 180 \text{ (max HR)} - 60 \text{ (RHR)} = 120 \text{ (max HR II)}$$

$$120 \times 70\% \text{ (lower end of moderate range)} = 84 + 60 \text{ (RHR)} = 144$$

$$120 \times 79\% \text{ (upper end of moderate range)} = 95 + 60 \text{ (RHR)} = 155$$

Therefore, if this man's RHR is 60, his target heart rate range for moderate workouts is 144 to 155, with the exact target depending on the workout selected. Note that these are a bit higher than those using the simple formula.

Women use a similar formula, substituting 226 for 220:

$$226 - \text{age} = \text{max HR} - \text{RHR} = \text{max HR II}$$

So, for a 30-year-old woman, the formula would work like this:

$$226 - 30 = 196 \text{ (max HR)} - 60 \text{ (RHR)} = 136 \text{ (max HR II)}$$

$$136 \times 70\% \text{ (lower end of moderate range)} = 95 + 60 \text{ (RHR)} = 155$$

$$136 \times 79\% \text{ (upper end of moderate range)} = 107 + 60 \text{ (RHR)} = 167$$

Therefore, if this woman's RHR is 60, her target heart rate range for moderate workouts is 155 to 167, with the exact target depending on the workout selected. Note that these are a bit higher than those using the simple formula and also higher than the man's because women's heart rates are usually faster because they are smaller.

Other Formulas

By no means are these the only ways to calculate a heart rate. If you read popular magazines, you'll see variations popping up all the time. They can be fun to experiment with to see how different they really are. In many cases the differences are so minimal that it comes down to splitting hairs, which is something advanced athletes like to do! The previous two formulas should give you enough of a range to start you off on the right foot.

Again, these calculations are only estimates; individuals vary greatly. As you gain experience, learn to pay more attention to how you feel—your perceived exertion—than to your heart rate as you estimate how hard you're working.

Rating Your Perceived Exertion

As you become accustomed to walking workouts, you'll learn to read your personal perceived exertion level, which is another way to measure how hard you're working without stopping to take a heart rate. Learning to gauge your exertion and to rate yourself requires listening to your body.

Measuring your rate of perceived exertion (RPE) can help you gauge how hard you're working. Generally, a person's sense of effort corresponds well to objective measurements such as percentages of maximum heart rate. An RPE of 1 to 3 has a corresponding heart rate of 55 to 69 percent of the maximum. A score of 4 to 5 has a corresponding heart rate of 70 to 79 percent of the maximum. A score of 6 to 8 has a corresponding heart rate of 80 to 94 percent of the maximum. Once they are highly trained, athletes can do short, intense workouts that push them to 10. The workouts in part II are arranged by type and progress in intensity as shown in table 4.3.

Speed is only one component that will affect your RPE. For example, if you walk with your dog, push a stroller, or carry some groceries, your walking speed may be decreased, but you will make up for some of this with the increased maneuvering difficulty, which will likely bump up your RPE a notch or two.

Table 4.3	Intensity Levels for Walking Workouts	
Workout type	**RPE**	**% max HR**
Short and easy	1-3	55-69
Medium and steady	3-4	65-74
Medium and quicker	4-6	70-84
Short and fast	5-7	75-89
Long and steady	5-8	75-94

Estimating Calories

As your workouts progress in intensity or length, the number of calories you use also goes up. Even if weight loss is one of your fitness goals, don't overdo your workouts with the goal to use more calories more quickly. Overloading your system too soon, at whatever level, can cause it to break down. With exercise, that means strains and pains that might put a stop not only to good exercise intentions but also to safe, gradual weight loss. Heed the tortoise's wisdom: Slow and steady wins the race.

The number of calories you use in a workout is the least of your worries, really, because it's usually not a huge amount. What counts is (1) teaching your system to use fat more efficiently as a primary fuel all of the time, which will decrease your body fat; (2) building muscle in place of fat, because muscle uses more calories than fat even at rest; and (3) letting your engine stay on high after a workout, as studies show it does. That means you'll use more calories just sitting in your car, for example, once you're more fit! And you'll use more calories in the first minutes and hours *after* a workout even though you're watching TV.

Be warned, too, that calorie expenditures vary greatly from person to person based on your individual metabolism, muscle mass, fat mass, and skill and fitness level. It also varies depending on the weather, terrain, and environment, as well as how hard you work during each workout. The estimates in table 4.4 are based on a 150-pound person. Add 15 percent to the totals for every 25 pounds over 150, and subtract 15 percent from the totals for every 25 pounds under 150. But, remember, these are only estimates.

Table 4.4   Caloric Costs of Walking

Level	Cal/mile	Total cal used
Short and easy	50-80	55-160
Medium and steady	80-90	140-390
Medium and quicker	90-100	130-420
Short and fast	90-100	135-300
Long and steady	90-100	270-1,300

Note: Calories used does not include warm-up, cool-down, walk options, or other exercises.

Estimating Distances

Many cities have trails that are marked every quarter mile, half mile, or full mile. These make setting up a walking routine pretty easy if you need to know or want to know distances versus time on your feet. If there are no marked areas, measure your courses by drive alongside your sidewalk route (remember, this is a very rough estimate), or buy an inexpensive pedometer or even a GPS (global positioning system) to measure your distance.

You can also do shorter workouts on a quarter-mile track. Once you get the feel of how fast you cover a certain distance, you can use time as your guide to measure distance. For example, walk 15 minutes one way, then 15 minutes back for a 2-mile round trip at a 4-mile-per-hour pace. Note that four laps around a track *only* in the *inside lane* is 1 mile; for every lane outside that, you're adding a short distance. In the outside lane, four laps equal about $1\frac{1}{8}$ miles. Pay attention to etiquette when you use a track. The inside two lanes are reserved for serious runners and walkers doing specific timed workouts (intervals) geared toward higher performance. Unless you need to time every lap you walk, fitness walkers and joggers belong in the outside lanes.

One more way to gauge your pace and distance is by counting how many steps you take per minute. Use table 4.5 as a guide. Remember, this too is only an estimate because stride lengths vary.

Table 4.5 Estimating Your Pace With Steps per Minute

Steps/min	Miles/hour	Min/mile
60-80	2-2.4	25-30
85-95	2.5-2.9	21-24
100-115	3-3.3	18-20
120-125	3.4-3.6	$16\frac{1}{2}$-$17\frac{1}{2}$
130-135	3.8-4	15-16
140-145	4.3-4.6	13-14
150-155	4.6-4.8	$12\frac{1}{2}$-13
160-165	5-5.2	$11\frac{1}{2}$-12
170+	>5.5	<11

Counting 10,000 Steps

Perhaps you've heard about walking 10,000 steps a day to good health. Let me explain briefly what that's all about. The suggestion to shoot for 10,000 steps is a great one because it addresses those looking for a little more movement as a part of their normal daily routine instead of a regular exercise program. The step count comes from an estimate that 2,000 steps is about 1 mile, so if you can attain 10,000 daily steps, you cover about 5 miles in a day. These steps usually will not raise your heart rate into moderate training zones.

To achieve a goal like this, you should not immediately go from zero movement, or zero steps, to 10,000 steps but instead progress gradually. You can count your steps by wearing a pedometer, a piece of gear discussed in chapter 3.

Although the programs in this book will improve your health like a step-counting program will, I also advocate adding general activity to your everyday life by taking the stairs or parking farther from your destination, activities that will help you reach the 10,000 steps goal. However, I also believe that if you are interested in fitness walking, you are interested in more structure and more focus on fitness training than counting steps provides. Of course, wearing a good pedometer can help you estimate workout distance. And it can be entertaining to see how many steps you normally take during your day.

Charting Your Progress

If you look at the black-and-white numbers of time and distance, then walking is one of many activities in which progress can be measured precisely. Measurement and log keeping are vital parts of any fitness program. But mental progress is also important.

The programs in this book are founded on two promises from you, the walker:

1. **Honesty.** You must always be true to yourself in assessing your personal ability, energy level, and needs, using only *you* as a yardstick, not a neighbor or friend. No workout is too slow, too short, or inadequate in any way. Every movement is a building block—accept it for what it is.

2. **Diligence.** Sticking to it is essential. Don't give up, no matter what. Fitness takes time, whether you're going from a sedentary lifestyle to working out three days a week or from brisk walking to serious power walking. Your body needs time to adjust, to build muscle, to learn to use fat more efficiently, and to increase lung and heart strength.

What is progress in a fitness program? Progress requires looking over the edge into the unknown chasm of human potential and depth of character, then jumping. It is a process of exploring what your body can do, at whatever fitness level you choose, then trying it. It requires following your dream, step by step, until you can reach your goal.

Making exercise a regular part of your life takes at least six weeks and up to six months to become a real habit. For a beginner, making it to the six-month mark is true progress and worthy of celebration. For more intermediate and advanced walkers, putting in additional effort to advance further is progress. Exercise will become an inspirational activity that will alter your mood from bad to good, your stress from high to nonexistent. When I'm out of sorts or tired, heading out for a workout is often the best medicine, even if I don't really feel like it. I almost always come back grateful that I pushed myself out the door. You will too.

Measurements must be made if you want to compare your workouts today with those from last week or last year. Make a copy of the training log in figure 4.2 on page 46. Use it to record your workouts and keep track of your progress. Things to note in the comments section include the location of your workout, the weather, and how you felt. Evaluate your progress three ways:

1. **Time.** You can retake the 1-mile walking test at any time (preferably not more than once a month) and compare your time with previous 1-mile walks. In your log book, observe how long it takes you to cover certain distances. Are you moving faster? Note if your workouts are becoming more challenging by getting longer. That's progress, too.

2. **Feelings.** You'll notice a space in the sample log to jot down a couple of words about how you felt. Were your legs heavy or light? Were they sore? Did they feel relaxed? Did the workout feel easy or as if the whole thing were uphill even if it was flat? Maybe you're going faster and farther, but it feels easier. All this relates to perceived exertion. Compare how you perceived your body during similar workouts in different weeks, as well as your rating of perceived exertion.

3. **Physical signs**. Your body will let you know what's going on—listen to it. Your resting heart rate is one concrete measure. Take it and record it often. As you gain fitness, your resting heart rate should go down. If it is suddenly higher than normal by 5 to 10 beats, that can signify overtraining, fatigue, stress, or an impending illness. Take heed and take a break.

If you've had your body fat tested (often available with calipers at clubs or using home versions that pinch your body fat at several specific sites), test it every month or two and note the changes. A scale is not a good judge because your body weight might stay the same or even go up, even though you lose fat and your clothes fit more loosely with consistent exercise. That's because muscle weighs more than fat. What about your blood tests? Your blood cholesterol, low-density lipoprotein, and triglyceride levels will likely go down. No matter what your body weight does, this is progress toward better health. Sleep patterns will also improve. You'll fall asleep more quickly, rest more soundly, and awaken more refreshed when you exercise. You'll also have more energy during the day.

You're done just reading about walking for now. You're ready to warm up, cool down, and dive into walking-specific stretching and strengthening exercises you can use before and after your workouts.

Sample Exercise Log

Date	Workout type/number	Total distance/time	Pace	Heart rate/effort	Comments
Tuesday May 5	SF5	3.5 miles, including warm-up/cool-down	15-min miles	130/4-5	It was a cool morning. Felt OK after my warm-up. Did extra. Was at local park. Maybe it's time to try faster paces?

Summary:

Figure 4.2 Sample exercise log.

CHAPTER **5**

Supplemental Routines and Activities

Your balanced and safe workout doesn't start and end with a brisk walk. It actually starts in your mind before you head out the door, continues with a slow warm-up, includes a few stretches (if needed), *then* kicks into gear at your chosen speed for the day's workout. Afterward, your routine should include additional stretches and then strengtheners. All of these components make up your entire routine from start to finish.

Flexibility exercises are an essential part of your walking routine and not an extra, optional, or alternative cross-training component. The same goes for strengthening, although these can be done anytime during the week and not necessarily after a walking workout. This chapter includes the specifics of muscle strengthening, with instruction for and illustrations of a short selection of exercises you can build into your walking program to play a supporting role.

Another important supplement to your walking program is cross-training activities. Walking is or will become your primary source of activity and your true passion. But every exerciser can find that other activities now and then refresh the mind and body. That's why I introduce a starter menu of activities later in this chapter that walkers can use to round out a program.

Warming Up Heart, Mind, and Muscles

When you begin a workout, every part of you needs to ease into it—certainly your muscles—but also your heart and your mind. A muscle after a day at work or a night's sleep is like cold taffy: Bend it, and it cracks, splinters, or snaps. When it's warm, it's soft and pliable.

A warm-up prepares your muscles for the activity to come, letting them rehearse in slow motion the way they'll move later. A warm-up for a walking workout can simply be walking slowly for about 5 minutes.

People sometimes talk about warm-up stretches. Actually, there's no such thing. There's a warm-up, and there are stretches. A warm-up should come first. Both are important when done at the right time, but the two in one breath contradict each other. The deepest of stretches—those aiming to improve flexibility and not just loosen muscles—come after your workout as part of the cool-down. I discuss these in the next section.

The warm-up itself should target your muscles, and that includes your heart, because it's a muscle too and also needs warming up. Those first 5 minutes of easy walking coax it into working a little harder. You wouldn't start your car's engine after it has sat in the cold overnight, throw the pedal to the metal, and roar down the street. You know that you have to give the engine time to warm up, allowing the fluids and gears to move freely as you slowly pick up speed. The same goes for your body's engine, the heart.

Then there's your mind, an important element in workout success. When you crawl out of bed or away from your desk after eight hours (or more), you probably don't feel like exercising vigorously or, for that matter, even moderately. Promise yourself at least 5 minutes. Give yourself permission to quit after 5 minutes if you don't feel like going on. Most likely, those first few minutes will change your mind, convincing you that the workout will feel good, and you'll keep going. That's one benefit of a warm-up right there: motivation to keep going. The warm-up also lets you tune in to twinges or aches. If you still feel them after the warm-up, take a cue and skip this workout. If it's not so bad after all, continue the workout but not so intensely. Listen to your body.

While you're striding through the active warm-up—the easy movement that comes before the stretches—take the time to roll your shoulders forward and backward, lift them to your ears and pull them down, drop your chin to your chest, move your head from side to side, flex your hands and shake out your arms. Next, especially for more intense walks, take a few minutes for light stretches to loosen your muscles. For easier walks, stretches after the warm-up are optional. Remember, the deep stretching happens after your workout. Loosening muscles before activity can include some of the same stretches you'll do later, but don't push the stretch to the point of tension or mild discomfort that I describe in the next section. There should be no pain or discomfort when you loosen up before a walk.

Cooling Down and Stretching Out

Avoid coming to a dead stop when you're done with your walking workout. Just as you had to allow your heart, mind, and muscles to get used to the idea that you were picking up the pace, you have to give them the same chance to realize you're slowing down. A cool-down is exactly what it says: cooling down your body after heating it up during a workout. Don't just jump into your car or into the shower. Let your system cool off and return gradually to its steady state. Repeat what you did in the warm-up. Walk slowly for about 5 minutes (or more if the workout was long and very intense), rolling your shoulders and shaking out your hands. *Now* you're ready to stretch deeply.

No fitness program can be well rounded without exercises for flexibility. Flexibility exercises should be the unquestioned finish for every walk, with additional stretching on rest days or as cross-training (see pages 59-66 for a thorough discussion of cross-training choices). Think also about doing casual or impromptu stretches, such as a back stretch while sitting at your desk or a calf stretch while waiting in the grocery checkout line.

If you don't stretch, walking, like any other activity, will slowly tighten the muscles in your buttocks (gluteal group), the backs of your thighs (hamstrings), and your calves (gastrocnemius). It's important to follow the flexibility exercises in this chapter to continue walking injury free and comfortably.

Muscles shorten as they tire during exercise. Stretching after a workout will return them to their preworkout length and perhaps teach them to be a little more flexible. Working out without stretching starts the snowball effect: You don't stretch because you're tight, but the less you stretch, the tighter you get! A tight muscle isn't only uncomfortable, it often signals weakness, and tightness and weakness set you up for strains and other injuries. After a workout, your muscles are pliable and ready to stretch without getting hurt. Follow three easy rules when you stretch:

1. Stretch until you feel tension and a mild discomfort, but not pain. Hold the stretch at this point and breathe deeply.

2. Don't bounce. Bouncing causes the muscles to protect themselves from overstretching by tightening. Yes, you'll actually tighten your muscles if you bounce.

3. Hold each stretch for 10 to 30 seconds to let the muscle relax. Continue to breathe deeply, and as the muscle releases, you'll be able to stretch a bit farther.

If you follow the popular media, perhaps you've heard about the 2004 journal article from researchers who said they found no proof that stretching reduced injuries. That research was a thorough, well-done review of past studies on stretching to assess that relationship. It concluded that stretching was not significantly associated with a reduction in injuries. However, it also said (and this is the part often left out) that there was not enough evidence to endorse *or* recommend discontinuing stretching exercises by active people before or after exercise, and it urgently called for more well-conducted studies to determine stretching's proper role in sports and exercise. So, the bottom line is, don't stop. Adding a few stretches won't hurt, and the review found that stretches did seem to show increased flexibility if held long enough. Stretching just may provide preventive medicine.

The following stretches will help you loosen up before and after your walks.

Hamstrings

Stand about 2 feet away from a bench or raised surface. Place your right leg on the bench, allowing your left leg to bend slightly. With your hands resting on your right thigh, lean forward, bending at the hips and keeping your spine extended without hunching. Reach forward with your chest and keep your chin from dropping to your chest. Repeat on the other side.

Hips, Back, and Buttocks

Sit on the ground with your legs extended forward. Bend your left leg and cross your left foot over your right knee, placing your left foot on the ground on the outside of your straight right knee or lower leg. Rest on your left hand beside and behind you for support. Wrap your right arm around your left knee and gently pull the knee toward you as you twist your head and torso in the direction of your left arm. Repeat on the opposite side.

Inner Thighs

Sit on the ground with your knees bent and the soles of your feet together. Grasp your ankles and lean forward, keeping your back straight as you stretch and trying to relax your knees downward. You can also sit with your back to a wall to help you into this stretch.

Thighs and Hip Flexors

Stand with your right hand against a flat surface (such as a wall or tree) for balance and support. Bend your left leg behind you, grasping the ankle with your left hand. Bend your right knee slightly to help keep you from swaying your back. Push your left foot backward into your hand while keeping the knee pointed toward the ground and your hips pressed forward. Repeat on the opposite side. Avoid this stretch if you have chronic knee pain. Also, avoid pulling your foot toward your buttocks, as this will place excessive strain on your knees.

Sides of Legs

Stand next to a wall about an arm's length away. Using your arm to support you, cross the leg farthest from the wall over the front of the leg nearest the wall. Push your hip toward the wall, keeping the leg nearest the wall straight while allowing the crossed leg to bend. Allow your supporting arm to bend as your hip reaches toward the wall. Repeat on the opposite side. Avoid turning or twisting your body toward or away from the wall.

Shins

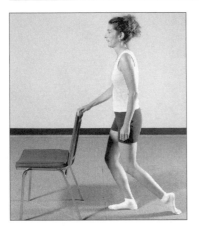

Place the top of the foot on the ground behind you and press your ankle toward the ground, allowing your knee to bend as you stretch. Repeat on the opposite side. This can also be done while sitting in a chair to achieve additional stretch through the front of your lower leg.

Calves

Face a wall with one foot close to the wall and one about two feet behind you. The knee of the back leg should remain straight with the heel on the ground. If you cannot maintain that position, bring the foot closer to the wall. The front leg should be bent at the knee in a lungelike position. Place your hands against the wall, and then bend your arms as you lean toward the wall, keeping your back straight and abdominals tight. To achieve a calf stretch, keep the rear heel on the floor. Repeat on opposite side. To stretch a different part of the calf, repeat above, but move the rear foot in slightly and bend the rear knee while still keeping the heel on the ground.

Back

Stand about 18 inches away from a wall or flat surface with your feet parallel to it. Turn toward the wall and place both hands on it at about chest height. Gently continue turning toward the wall, using your fingers to crawl along the wall, reaching behind you. Repeat on the opposite side.

Low Back

Lie flat on your back. Bend your knees and bring them toward your chest while grasping behind your thighs. Pull your knees toward your shoulders until your hips come off the ground. After holding the stretch, extend your legs slowly, one at a time. You can also do this stretch with one knee at a time pulled toward your chest. If you have back problems, check with your doctor first.

Chest

Stand with your back to a wall. Reach back and place one of your palms on the wall with your wrist facing out and your arm outstretched at shoulder height. Gently turn your head and chest away from the wall as far as you can. Repeat on the opposite side.

Strengthening and Toning

No fitness program can be considered well rounded without exercises to increase muscle strength. Because of the vigorous arm swing, walking tones upper-body muscles more than running (good distance-running form demands that participants carry their arms more passively, which achieves little if any muscle conditioning). Walking's arm movement and upper-back engagement isn't enough, though, to keep bones healthy and muscles strong for the rest of life's demands.

As you fine-tune your overall fitness program, try to find time for two muscle-toning sessions a week, as recommended by the American College of Sports Medicine (ACSM). Target large muscle groups from head to toe. Exercise 8 to 10 muscle groups, twice a week, performing 8 to 12 repetitions of each. Such a toning routine doesn't require more than 20 to 30 minutes, although you can always do more if you want. Remember, exercises to strengthen muscles need not be complicated or expensive.

Weight Machines

Often called *selectorized* machines because you select a weight by moving a pin in a stack of weight blocks, these are the machines you normally see at clubs. In a club, one machine is usually used for one exercise, such as a hamstring curl. For home use, you'll find units that combine an entire range of exercises on one compact station that can, depending on the design, use any combination of seats, pins, pulleys, stacks, bars, or cables. One stack means it's available for one user at a time, while two-stack home gyms can be used by two people at once. Since the mid- to late-1990s, home gyms have become very advanced and can be a great investment that offers about all you need, especially if you can't, won't, or don't want to go to a local club.

Free Weights

Rather than stacks of weight attached to cables or pins, free weights are dumbbells and barbells, which are bars on which you slide plates of weight on the ends to create the weight you need to lift, push, or pull. The beauty of free weights is their adaptability; add a simple bench—one that can decline or incline or has a bar and stand for bench presses—and you can do just about anything. The only catch is, you have to know what to do and how to do it. If you don't, your workouts won't achieve what you want them to, or worse, you might hurt yourself. And you always run the risk of becoming frustrated and quitting. Free weights are best if you have experience or knowledge or will read a book to learn an appropriate program and proper technique. You can also hire a personal trainer for a couple of sessions who can help set up a program for you.

Rubber Resistance and Body Weight

Weight machines and free weights are great for building strength and toning, but if your goal is basic conditioning, there are cheaper and simpler options. You can also use rubber resistance tubes and bands, work against your own body weight, or invest in a stability ball or balance board. You can do abdominal exercises and push-ups on your living room floor, and pulling on inexpensive rubber surgical tubing or bands is a fine substitute for using a weight machine to condition muscles in the back, chest, arms, legs, and feet. Those large, inflated stability balls usually come with enough illustrated instruction to get you started on basic overall exercises and stretches. And balance boards can strengthen and condition your lower legs and abdominals even more. None of this equipment costs much and they are compact (well, other than the ball);

just stick them in a drawer or under your bed. The ball, by the way, is a great office or TV-watching chair that can help you sit up straight and use your abs while just sitting there!

Walking-Specific Exercises

Proper strengthening should balance the strength between muscle groups as well as target areas that may be susceptible for tightness or that need extra strength for a particular activity. For example, if you strengthen the quadriceps, don't forget the hamstrings; if you work the chest, be sure to also work your back. If your low back tends to tire or ache, focus on your abs as well as your back, but first consult with your doctor. Be aware that walking uses the shins and calves, so be sure to work these areas.

Certainly a well-rounded strengthening and toning program is best and allows you to hit all parts of your body. The following basic selection of exercises provides a whole-body approach to major muscle groups. But don't be constrained by this list. It's just a start. There are hundreds of different exercises and a thousand different ways to do them. This group focuses on those you can do at home without extensive or expensive machines or equipment. One key for all exercises is to avoid holding your breath during the movement. Don't laugh. You'd be amazed how many people take a final gulp and hold it as if they're going underwater. Breathe!

A health club trainer or a thorough book specifically on strengthening will help you develop a larger repertoire of exercises. Meanwhile, these will get you started.

Overall Upper Body (Push-Ups)

Many people have bad memories of gym classes and presidential tests, but this is an easy overall upper-body toner and strengthener. And, compared to gym class where you got yelled at if you stopped, you can actually do short sets and rest.

Lie on the floor, facedown. Place your hands under your shoulders. You can either lift your body by straightening your elbows but leaving your knees on the ground, or place your toes on the ground and lift your body into the air into a straight boardlike position. Whichever you choose, keep your abdominals tight, don't let your back sag or sway, and keep your head and neck aligned with your back rather than letting it drop toward the ground. Next, lower your chest toward the ground while bending your elbows, and then lift yourself back up to a straight-arm position. Repeat as many times as you can before your position and technique disintegrate. Rest. Repeat.

Abdominals I (Crunches)

Lie on the ground flat on your back. Bend your knees so that your feet are flat on the floor. Either cross your arms over your chest or rest your head in your hands, using your hands only to support the head. Do not yank on your head. Lift your torso and imagine shortening the distance between the bottom of your ribs and the top of your hips. Keep your head back, eyes on the ceiling and elbows open. Think about pulling your belly button into the floor and exhaling as you lift. Keep your abs from bulging outward by emphasizing the contraction during the entire lift. Lower slowly.

Abdominals II (Sides)

This works the muscles in your sides called obliques that help to support your back, tighten your waist, and hold in the abdominal muscles in the front. Lie on the ground flat on your back. Bend your knees so that your feet are flat on the floor. Put your hands behind your head, resting your head in your hands. Lift your torso up, turn toward one side, aiming your arm pit at the opposite knee and keeping the elbow back, then return to the straight position, and lower slowly. Again, exhale as you lift and inhale as you lower. Keep your abs from bulging outward by concentrating on the contraction during the entire lift. Repeat on the other side.

Upper Back

Strengthening your upper- and middle-back muscles will help you stand tall and make your arm swing stronger, too. To work your upper back, hold a long and wide elastic band, such as a Dynaband or Thera-Band, or rubber tubing, with one end in each hand. Keep the band taut. Raise your arms over your head (pretend you're forming a Y), but keep your shoulders down and relaxed. Pull down and slightly outward, with your elbows lowering toward the ground and the band moving behind your head. Focus on your upper-back muscles. Raise slowly to the overhead start position. Repeat 10 to 12 times.

Middle Back

Sit down on a chair or on the floor. Loop an elastic band around the back of an object in front of you. You can also tie the band to a door handle, forming two tails to grab that are a couple of feet long. Grab each end with your arms extended and your hands directly in front of your chest. Try this with the palms facing down and with the palms facing in. Pull back  on the band so that your elbows reach behind you, and focus on squeezing and working the muscles in the middle of your back and shoulder blades. Slowly return your hands to the start position. Repeat 8 to 12 times.

Low Back

Lie facedown on the floor with your hands under your shoulders, as if you were getting ready to do a push-up. Slowly lift your chest and shoulders off the floor, keeping your chin down (don't yank your head back or touch it to your chest). Keep your abdominal muscles tight, and only extend as far as is comfortable without straining or pushing hard with your hands. Hold and  breathe for 10 to 20 seconds. Exhale and release slowly to the ground. Release your arms to your side and relax for a minute. Repeat two to five times.

Lunges

Stand with both feet together, giving yourself at least 4 feet of open space in front of you. Keep your abdominals tight, shoulders back, and spine aligned. Carefully step forward 3 to 4 feet with one foot. When that foot touches down, continue bending that knee into a slight lunge. Keep knee aligned over the foot rather than going past the toes. Your back knee will bend slightly and the heel will come up off the ground. Hold for a split second, then use your leg and foot to push you back into the starting position. Repeat 8 to 10 times. Repeat with the  other leg. You can also hold hand weights. If you have knee problems or pain, avoid lunges or don't bend the knee deeply enough to cause pain.

Hamstrings

The hamstrings in the back of the upper leg also get a strong workout in walking. Stand facing a chair or other support with a circular rubber band or tube looped around your left ankle. Stand on the other end of the tube with your right foot, bending the knee slightly. Keeping your back straight and abdominals tight, lift your left until you feel the muscles in the back of your leg being used. Lower the foot just a little until the muscle relaxes, then pull the heel upward again. Work up to 10 to 12 repetitions with each leg.

Shins

The shins (the muscles in the front of your lower leg) get a particularly strong workout during walking because they're responsible for repetitively lifting the toe. When you first start walking, you might feel burning or extra fatigue in the shins. If you ice them before and after walks and stretch and strengthen them, these sensations will go away. Meanwhile, do a few strengtheners.

Attach a circular elastic band to the leg of a chair or table. Sit on the ground facing the band with your legs nearly straight. Hook the toes of one foot inside the loop of the band. Keep the band taut while you flex your foot, bringing the toe toward you. Keeping the band taut, slowly point your foot away from you. Do 15 to 20 repetitions per foot. Do several repetitions in which you flex your foot, as above, but then move your toes to the outside or inside before you relax into the pointed position. Repeat on the other side.

Calves

Stand with your toes on a step or curb. You may want to stand next to something you can hold onto to help you keep your balance. Lower your heels very slowly and carefully, and only to the point of a slight stretch or feeling of tension. Keep your abdominals tight and your shoulders back, rise up on your toes and lower again. Repeat 10 to 20 times.

Feet and Toes

It's amazing how important feet and toes are, yet how ignored they are. Try these towel scrunchers. Put a dishtowel or other thin cloth on the floor. Place your bare foot on top of the cloth and curl your toes while trying to grab the towel and move it or bunch it up. Do this for 15 seconds to a minute with each foot, building gradually.

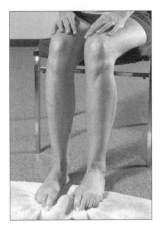

The wide rubber bands and tubes I mention are available in fitness specialty stores or other sporting good stores and usually come in various colors that represent different resistances. They often come in variety packs. The loops used for your feet are narrower, thicker, and made of tougher rubber, but if you can't find premade loops, use a high-resistance band and tie it into a loop. Check rubberized gear each time you use it to make sure there are no weak spots, cracks, or tears that could cause the band to break and snap in your face. Storing your bands out of the sun or heat will help them last longer.

Cross-Training

Cross-training is just a fancy term for mixing up and balancing your fitness activities. Think of it as fitness grazing. It should be fun and keep your body healthy and your mind alert. More and more people are discovering cross-training and consider it a part of their routine and not anything special. According to a 1992 national poll conducted for *Outside* magazine, the number of Americans who participated in more than one activity was expected to jump in 10 years by 73 percent, outpacing even the impressively increasing numbers of walkers. Taking a look around, I'll bet that growth has been reached.

Even as a walking aficionado, you should sample other activities for several reasons. First, you will strengthen and tone muscles that walking doesn't target. Walking requires the concentrated use of the muscles in the back of the leg, which can cause strength and flexibility imbalances. Cross-training can resolve possible imbalances.

Multiple activities also can generate added enthusiasm for exercise in general and walking specifically. Trying a smattering of activities will keep your mind and your body interested in exercise and will promote lifelong participation. Interest and ability in other activities can give you something to fall back on in case of an injury, travel, or other life and schedule changes. If you need, or are forced, to take a few days or more off from walking, you'll know how to substitute other activities so you can maintain your health, fitness, and vitality. Once you look around, you'll realize there is an array of activities you can add to your program, either now and then, seasonally, or just as the whim strikes. The following are a few activities that might be more interesting to a walker and the reasons to choose one or another. Remember, the choices don't stop here, so let this sample tickle your imagination.

To help you better sort out what you might want to choose, the activities are divided into two sections. The first includes a sampler of aerobic activities that are walking oriented in some way, but are still considered cross-training because they use different muscles, and the impact is varied. The second includes alternate nonwalking aerobic activities.

Variations of Walking

Walking itself can be transformed into a cross-training routine by adding equipment, diversifying your route, or changing your walking style. That's because the variation, just like cross-training techniques mentioned earlier, uses different muscles to create a nearly different workout, allowing some muscles to rest while stressing other less frequently used muscles. You can also use walking variations in special circumstances, for example, if you travel to a snowy resort for a vacation or to a mountain town on holiday or business travel. Here are a few varieties that may pique your interest.

Nordic Walking

Much like cross-country skiing but without skis or snow, Nordic walking uses lighter poles with different hand grips and emulates a cross-country-skiing style of push-off with the poles. A participant uses rubber tips on pavement and metal tips on dirt. Only introduced in the United States in 2003, the activity stems from Scandinavia (hence, the name) and is similar to pole walking that has been done for years in the United States with a slightly different style. Nordic walking can, depending on the user and his or her skill and technique, use about 20 percent more calories than regular walking. Plus, poling along demands more from back, chest, and arm muscles, so it turns into an upper-body workout too. You can also hone your cross-country ski technique. This is one fitness activity that had its birthplace in Europe, where it has become an

Nordic walking adds an additional challenge to a typical walking workout.

international phenomenon in just a couple of years with several million now participating in Nordic walking.

Retro Walking

This odd-sounding activity is no more than walking backward. Retro walking demands more energy than forward walking, reduces impact to nearly zero, and changes the pattern of muscle use to increase the demand on the quadriceps in the front of the thigh. Try short stretches (with one eye over your shoulder) on flat trails or uncrowded tracks. But attempt only short distances at a time because you don't want to back into anything. You'll find your stride will be shorter. Other than that, the only things to watch out for are obstacles.

Run-Walking

Maybe you like the feeling of bobbing along at a jog, but you don't like the impact. Try interspersing your walks with short runs of 1 to 2 minutes or whatever's comfortable. A more advanced walker can turn the runs into short sprints; an intermediate walker can make the run slow and easy and use it as a rest from fast walking. Beginners, however, should stick with walking. In addition, if you walk a lot of hills, you'll find that walking steep downhills can be difficult and even jarring. Sometimes, an easy jog down an incline is easier on your body. So try mixing up the run and walk portions based on terrain fluctuations.

Snowshoeing

This is really nothing more than winter walking. And what a beautiful thing it is! No special technique is needed, although you might need time to get used to the snowshoes. Snowshoeing can use more calories and muscles and gets you outdoors or into the woods, perhaps to explore areas that are impassable in regular shoes. Even if you don't live in a snowy area, you may travel some-place that is or live near mountain areas where snowshoeing is an alternative to a fitness walk. The technology in snowshoes has advanced, so the gear you may have in mind—big woven baskets—is archaic at best. Today's snowshoes are smaller, lighter, designed to make gripping on uphills and downhills easier and safer, and are even gender specific. If you don't want to buy a pair, you can rent them at outdoor and ski shops for day or weekend outings.

Outdoor Circuit Training

So you don't have time to get to a health club? Transform the outdoors into your own gym by looking at variations in the environment as places to challenge your muscles. Do step-ups on curbs or low benches. Walls or fences are great for push-ups. Try triceps dips on planters or benches (put yourself in a face-up "crab walk" position with the palms of your hands on the planter or bench, then bend and straighten your elbows). Jump up and touch signs or low branches as you move along. Hop over low obstacles, even repetitively. In between all those, keep on walking. It's like your very own outdoor gym circuit.

You can even carry rubber tubes or bands to add resistance exercises to your personalized routine. Walking with hand weights (addressed in chapter 3) isn't worth the potential for injury, however. The same goes for ankle weights, which also throw off your body mechanics and can strain your joints.

Aerobic Activities

Walking may be your first choice for cardiovascular fitness, and that's great because it's adaptable. But other activities can round out your exercise menu. As usual, aim for a minimum of 20 minutes of any activity. Don't limit yourself to the activities I've highlighted here, although these offer certain advantages as a supplement to walking, which I note. Otherwise, the sky's the limit!

Outdoor Bicycling

A bicycle can offer freedom to see areas your feet can't take you to. The movement can also be a relief from walking's repetitive heel-toe routine. A great leg strengthener, the cycling action creates no impact on the joints and uses more of your quadriceps than walking does. And you can still get outside to watch the world go by. Thirty minutes of cycling at a steady 15 miles per hour (mph) uses nearly the same amount of energy as walking for 30 minutes at 4.5 mph.

Group Exercise

Since its dance-oriented beginnings, aerobics has evolved into a wide variety of group exercise classes. Something is available to match every taste, not to mention every coordination level. These include low-impact, step training, circuit and interval classes, dance, and weight training (sometimes using a variety of names such as body sculpting or toning). Classes held indoors are a handy alternative to walks in inclement weather, and one session can work out your whole body. Trendy music adds a fun element, too. Don't overlook water aerobics or aqua step classes as possibilities. There are even indoor cycling classes. Of course, you can also pop in a tape or DVD and turn your living room into a private studio for a quick workout at your convenience.

Most hour sessions will include 30 to 35 minutes of aerobics plus 10 minutes of warm-up and stretching and 5 to 10 minutes of cool-down and stretching. As with cycling, 30 minutes of low-impact aerobics, not including the warm-up and cool-down, uses about the same number of calories as walking 30 minutes at 4.5 mph.

Indoor Equipment

The incredible variety in indoor exercise equipment means you should be able to find an enjoyable form of cross-training. Depending on your needs as a walker, you can choose equipment at a club or for your home to emphasize walking muscles (treadmills, steppers, and elliptical trainers), to emphasize opposing muscles (bicycles and rowing machines), or to train the whole body (ladderlike climbers, cross-country ski machines, and dual-action bicycles).

Indoor workouts let you distract yourself with television, movies, or reading—or simply offer a change of pace. They also allow you to stay home without missing your workout if you have a child to watch or a telephone call to wait for. They can also provide a safe way to work out before dawn or after dark.

On most indoor equipment, you may feel as if you're working harder than you would during a walk. Let your body tell you how long the workout should be. Twenty to thirty minutes on most equipment will give you a good workout, but you can lengthen the workout as needed or desired. If you're at a club, make your workout more interesting by working out on three different pieces of equipment for 10 minutes each.

Swimming

Swimming uses more muscles in the upper body, in contrast to walking's nearly exclusive use of lower-body muscles. It also promotes flexibility where walking and other upright activities tend to tighten muscles. Walkers don't need much of a break from impact, but swimming's fluid cushion eliminates pounding or strain from gravity. Immersion in water can soothe the body as well as the mind, adding a peaceful alternative to street walks.

Swim laps steadily for 30 minutes for a workout equivalent to walking 30 minutes at 4 mph.

Hiking

Walking doesn't necessarily mean on city streets and around your neighborhood or local park like a robot. Walking can also mean heading for the great outdoors and hitting your stride on dirt trails. You may not go as fast or as evenly paced as on pavement, but walking on uneven surfaces, such as dirt or gravel, adds an additional conditioning element for your lower legs and feet. It creates the need for your foot and lower legs to keep you upright and sparks proprioception, which means your muscles and nervous system are training to keep you balanced. Plus, you'll be forced to move your body in different ways as you go up and down hills or over and around rocks or trees, all providing more balanced muscular training.

An additional benefit of hiking is, of course, getting out into nature, which is something you can enjoy either by yourself, with a walking partner, or with your family. Because walking uphill is more difficult and energy intensive, depending on the softness of the terrain, it can use 50 percent more calories. So if you take a hike, you may need to go more slowly, cover less distance, or take extra breaks. Outdoors, breaks give you a chance to smell the flowers and trees and observe wildlife, which are great additions to your program.

Water Running or Walking

Running and walking aren't just for land. You can do either in the water to relieve impact. When you walk or run in water, the higher the water comes on your body, the more difficult your workout will be because you have to push through more resistance. Another workout to consider is deep-water running, where your feet don't touch the bottom of the pool. Instead you are suspended and experience no impact while emulating a running movement. This is a great workout if you have a lower-body injury or just to feel the massage of the water. For intense deep-water running, a specially made flotation belt helps you stay afloat, allowing you to focus on your technique. Water running and walking workouts can be great cooling retreats in the summer, as well as warming retreats in a heated pool in the winter.

If you take your heart rate during a water workout, note that the number you see will be lower by 10 to 15 percent than your reading on land. Researchers aren't sure why, but they think it has to do with the water's resistance on your body helping pump the blood.

A walking workout in the water can be a welcome change of pace and environment.

© Aqua Jogger

Yoga, Pilates, or Tai Chi

Other superior cross-training activities fall under the umbrella of mind–body fitness. You likely know them as practices called yoga, Pilates, or tai chi. All have become more popular since the late 1990s. Many clubs offer these stretching, meditative, focused, strengthening activities, sometimes in various combinations. Because of the peaceful, inner focus and the lengthening of the muscles involved, a mind–body fitness activity is a super addition to any fitness program, but especially to one that contracts muscles, such as walking. Yoga can, for example, increase flexibility, but it can also build considerable strength, and some types are quite aerobic. Pilates is mostly a strengthener, particularly of your abdominal and core muscles, which can be a great asset to walking. Tai chi is a softer and lighter activity but, with practice, can also raise your heart rate as well as build strength. Before you add these activities, you need some kind of instruction, be it at a studio or from a home video. These Eastern-influenced classes can be a wonderful multilevel cross-training component of your walking routine.

Cross-Country Skiing

Just because you live someplace where it snows or you travel someplace snowy doesn't mean you have to sigh and give up your walking program. If you'd like something a little more technical than snowshoeing, try cross-country skiing. The easy striding (classic) form is much like fast walking in the way you use your arms, legs, and hips. The more advanced skating form is more difficult but could become a good cross-training tool because it demands significant balance and stability, not to mention extensive use of the hip and gluteal muscles.

Running or Jogging

Perhaps you can't or don't want to run, which may be why you are getting into fitness walking. If so, skip this section. But I prefer not to be a "walking snob," just as I take offense at "running snobs." One activity doesn't have to preclude the other, and in fact, they complement each other. For example, taking an easy run or jog a couple of times a week, jogging for your cool-down, or run-walking (alternating running and walking) can be a nice way to let your walking muscles relax. Running and walking use different muscles, so adding in a bit of running is cross-training. Do not be afraid to try it if it's comfortable.

This list barely scratches the surface. In my list, I've focused on the most basic and most common. Others include golf, tennis, orienteering, paddling, skateboarding, and even ballroom dancing! Now's the time to charge right into the recommended workouts, all of which can be easily tailored or mixed and matched to suit your needs and level.

The Workouts

This section on workouts is what makes this book special. Workouts are arranged by type, based on duration, speed, and intensity. That makes it easy for you to choose your workouts, mix and match types, and keep track of your progress. The shortest and easiest workouts, called simply *short and easy*, help novice exercisers or health walkers get the feel for moving, while more experienced walkers can use these as easy days in a complete walking program. Those are grouped in chapter 6. In chapter 7 the workouts progress to *medium and steady*, because they aren't really long, nor are they fast, but are done at a steady pace without breaks. I like to call this moderate style "walking with intent." You may also call them brisk. The workouts in chapter 8 are called *medium and quicker,* which may sound odd at first, but listen up: These aren't any longer than the previous type but are quicker than "easy" and even a bit quicker than "steady" but without being speedy or exhausting; these are more like walking as if you're late for a bus or appointment. In these, you add a bit of snap to your step and push just a bit harder than you might normally in a brisk, steady walk. These three types of workouts will form the meat of a walking program for most health and fitness walkers and even much of a balanced program for athletic walkers.

Next comes the fun part for those who want to try a bit more, either regularly or every now and then—the workouts that go beyond the basics and provide a satisfying challenge. Chapter 9 outlines *short and fast* workouts for people who have been walking regularly. They build speed using several types of training methods. These workouts are not meant for novices or those new to an exercise program such as health walkers. The last few workouts in this short and fast group are advanced. The final category contains *long and steady* workouts. These aren't necessarily fast but are meant to be longer than your normal workouts and can be tried once every week or two. The latter workouts are quite long and only for someone with at least a few months of foundation in walking. The other workouts encourage you to challenge your speed over a longer distance.

Of course, whether an easy workout is the main workout or a warm-up, or whether a long workout is actually long or just another easy workout depends on your level. Nevertheless, I have grouped easy workouts together, whether they are 1 mile or 4 miles. The same goes for quicker, upbeat walks. For some walkers a 15-minute mile may be very quick, while for others a walk won't feel quick until it pushes 11- or 12-minute miles.

Within each chapter, the level, length, and intensity advances from beginning to end so you can easily find where you belong. A summary chart at the beginning of each section lays out the basics of each workout so you can use it as a menu. It summarizes the components of the workout: total workout time with warm-up and cool-down but without stretching or strengthening time, total walk time without warm-up and cool-down, distance, and intensity (both heart rate and perceived effort). The total workout time includes plentiful warm-up and cool-down time. Try not to skimp here, but if you really need to, eliminate a couple of minutes or just start and finish more slowly.

Now, about those calorie counts you'll find on each workout. Remember that they are calculated using an average and are only meant to provide a ballpark figure. I've used a 150-pound person for these estimates, so you must make adjustments if you weigh more or less, about 15 percent for every 25 pounds. However, these counts can also vary significantly depending on the weather, your body composition, and other factors, as I discuss in chapter 4. And, as I also mention, the calories you use per workout can be much less important than how you are training your body to use energy and calories in the long run.

Now you're ready to start walking. Each chapter introduces and describe its specific types of workouts and requirements in more detail. Don't forget to do the warm-up and cool-down incorporated into each workout. Also refer to the detailed information about warm-ups, cool-downs, stretching, and strengthening in chapter 5. Each of these training components is important for developing a safe exercise program you can incorporate into your life and maintain for a lifetime.

Once you are familiar with the workouts, feel free to adapt the speeds to your own tastes or needs. Focus on how hard you're working, not on how fast you're walking.

On your mark, get set, . . . go!

Conversions for Common Kilometer Distances to Miles

Kilometers	Miles	Kilometers	Miles
3	1.86	15	9.3
5	3.1	20	12.4
8	5	30	18.6
10	6.2	42	26.2
12	7.5	50	31.1

6

Short and Easy Workouts

Short and easy workouts are just what you think: short and easy. They are the least demanding in both intensity and length. These workouts are intended to be easily accomplished and not overly strenuous. Although short and easy, you should be able to walk a mile without taking a break in about 20 to 25 minutes before you attempt one. If that's a bit of a stretch for you, take a look at the first two workouts; these introductory workouts will let you get used to working out before moving forward. If you can already walk that distance at that pace, you can skip the first two samples and choose your favorites and best-suited workouts from the other 10.

Short and easy workouts have several uses:

- During the first few weeks, those new to exercise and walking may design their programs entirely from these workouts.
- Health walkers beyond the true novice stage can create a program that consists mostly of these workouts. Beginners may, however, choose workouts from another category once or twice a week.
- Fitness and athletic walkers (intermediate and advanced walkers) can use these as easy days before or after longer or more intense workouts or as a way to stay in shape while traveling.
- Anyone recovering from injury or trying to restart an exercise program, walking or otherwise, can use these programs to meet their needs.
- Since these workouts are easy to fit into a break or lunch hour, someone trying to add small bouts of activity throughout the day may find these fit their needs nicely. Low intensity might mean less sweat and getting back to work easier from a quick jaunt.

Throughout this section, the distance covered increases gradually, usually by only a quarter mile per workout, and focuses on ¾ of a mile to 2 miles. Your rate of perceived exertion (RPE), which is explained in chapter 4, remains low, 2 to 3 on the RPE scale of 0 to 10, once you get past the first two introductory workouts. That's equivalent to 60 to 69 percent of your maximum heart rate (max HR). These workouts will last about 20 to 35 minutes, not including warm-up and cool-down. (If you are slipping one of these into a lunch hour or other break, you can just use the first few minutes as a warm-up and the last few as your cool-down.)

To be clear, let's define an easy walk: This is a strolling but steady pace—one that will allow you to smell the flowers without pressure to achieve a particular time or constantly check your watch. In the first workouts, be flexible. Stop to take a breather if you need to. Be gentle on yourself, allowing your body to get used to the simple walking motion. Think "easy does it." During the next 10 workouts, you'll also think easy but steady, without breaks and at a continuous pace. Find the speed you can maintain within the given range and stride off the distance. The only challenge is holding a steady pace. Speed is not a concern, although if you can't maintain 20- to 25-minute miles (2.4 to 3 mph), you should consider sticking with the preliminary two workouts before moving on.

You will not necessarily expend many calories in these workouts, but you will prime your body for longer and more intense workouts (if you want), and they will use more energy. You'll also prime your mind for longer and brisker walks. Either way, you will begin to gain health benefits from your first step forward. As the U.S. government stated in the mid-1990s and has reiterated: Just 30 minutes of moderate exercise, such as a steady walk, can reap immediate health rewards. So remember that all calorie estimates are just that—estimates.

Table 6.1 Preview: Short and Easy Workouts

Workout	Distance (miles)	Total workout time (min)	Walking time (min)	Intensity (% max HR/RPE)
1	¾	30-35	19-23	55-65/1-2
2	1	35-40	26-31	60-65/2
3	¾	30-35	19-23	55-65/2
4	1	35-40	25-30	65-69/3
5	1¼	35-45	26-29	60-65/2
6	1½	45-50	31-34	60-65/2
7	1¾	50	36-37	60-69/2-3
8	1¼	35-45	25-26	60-69/2-3
9	1½	35-45	30-31	60-69/2-3
10	1½	40-45	27-30	60-69/2-3
11	1¾	45-55	32-35	60-69/2-3
12	2	50-55	38	65-69/3

Workout 1

Total time: 30 to 35 minutes

Warm-up: Roll your shoulders and march in place, or walk around an open space easily for 3 to 5 minutes, then stretch if desired.

Workout

Distance	¾ mile
Walking time	19 to 23 minutes
Pace	25- to 30-minute miles
Heart zone	55 to 65% max HR
Effort	RPE 1 to 2

Cool-down: Walk around an open area or march in place, rolling your shoulders and shaking out your hands and arms, for 3 to 5 minutes, then stretch.

Calories used: 53

Comments: The time allotted for this workout allows only a couple of short rest stops. Make sure you can accomplish this without becoming overly breathless or very sore the next day before moving on to workout 3 and beyond.

Workout 2

Total time: 35 to 40 minutes

Warm-up: Roll your shoulders and march in place, or walk around an open space easily for 3 to 5 minutes, then stretch if desired.

Workout

Distance	1 mile
Walking time	26 to 31 minutes
Pace	25- to 30-minute miles
Heart zone	60 to 65% max HR
Effort	RPE 2

Cool-down: March in place or circle your yard, living room, or any open space for 3 to 5 minutes, rolling your shoulders and shaking out your arms and hands before stopping to stretch.

Calories used: 70

Comments: This mile should be covered with only a couple of short breaks. You should be able to complete it without a struggle. Do you have it down? Now you're ready to move on to the following workouts without breaks.

Workout 3

Total time: 30 to 35 minutes

Warm-up: Walk easily back and forth or for a short distance for 4 to 5 minutes, then stretch if desired.

Workout

Distance	¾ mile
Walking time	19 to 23 minutes
Pace	25- to 30-minute miles
Heart zone	55 to 65% max HR
Effort	RPE 2

Cool-down: Circle an open space for 4 to 5 minutes, shaking out your shoulders and hands before stopping to stretch.

Calories used: 56

Comments: Make sure your ¾-mile walk in workout 1 is successful before trying this. Remember that the goal is to maintain a steady, light-intensity walk without breaks.

Workout 4

Total time: 35 to 40 minutes

Warm-up: Walk easily around an open area at the start of your route for 4 to 5 minutes, then stretch if desired.

Workout

Distance	1 mile
Walking time	25 to 30 minutes
Pace	25- to 30-minute miles
Heart zone	65 to 69% max HR
Effort	RPE 3

Cool-down: Stroll lightly, lifting and lowering your shoulders to relieve tension for 4 to 5 minutes, then stretch.

Calories used: 75

Comments: Shoot for the low end in walking time, still keeping your perceived exertion light. You can repeat this workout several times, gradually getting a little faster over a period of a few weeks, dropping from 30 minutes to 25 minutes for the workout. Once you can complete the mile in 24 to 25 minutes, you're ready to move on to the next group of workouts.

Workout 5

Total time: 35 to 45 minutes

Warm-up: Walk easily for 4 to 5 minutes, then stretch if desired.

Workout

Distance	1¼ miles
Walking time	26 to 29 minutes
Pace	20- to 22-minute miles
Heart zone	60 to 65% max HR
Effort	RPE 2

Cool-down: Walk easily for 4 to 5 minutes, shaking out your arms, then stretch.

Calories used: 100

Comments: Notice that the pace picks up slightly as the distance increases. You should be able to hold this easily and steadily so that you feel as if you're moving well but aren't exhausted.

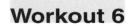

Workout 6

Total time: 45 to 50 minutes

Warm-up: Walk easily for 4 to 5 minutes, then stretch if desired.

Workout

Distance	1½ miles
Walking time	31 to 34 minutes
Pace	20- to 22-minute miles
Heart zone	60 to 65% max HR
Effort	RPE 2

Cool-down: Walk easily for 4 to 5 minutes, dropping your chin forward and your head from side to side to relax your neck, then stretch.

Calories used: 120

Comments: This workout challenges you to stay closer to a 21-minute mile. Listen to your body, though, and go more slowly if it demands it. Repeat this workout until you can master 20 or 21 minutes.

Workout 7

Total time: 50 minutes

Warm-up: Walk easily for 4 to 5 minutes, then stretch if desired.

Workout	
Distance	1¾ miles
Walking time	36 to 37 minutes
Pace	20-minute miles
Heart zone	60 to 69% max HR
Effort	RPE 2 to 3

Cool-down: Walk easily for 4 to 5 minutes, dropping your chin forward and your head from side to side to relax your neck, then stretch.

Calories used: 140

Comments: Try to step a bit faster, this time edging closer to a 20-minute mile, while still allowing yourself several rest stops. The goal is to complete the distance.

Workout 8

Total time: 35 to 45 minutes

Warm-up: Walk easily for about 5 minutes, then stretch if desired.

Workout

Distance	1¼ miles
Walking time	25 to 26 minutes
Pace	20- to 21-minute miles
Heart zone	60 to 69% max HR
Effort	RPE 2 to 3

Cool-down: Walk easily for 4 to 5 minutes, letting the front of your foot flap down onto the ground to relax your shins, then stretch.

Calories used: 100

Comments: As you pick up your pace, you might need more warm-up. Don't shortchange the easy warm-up walk and loosening stretches (look for those suggestions in chapter 5). They can make or break your workout, not to mention your comfort and ability to stay injury free.

Workout 9

Total time: 35 to 45 minutes

Warm-up: Walk easily for about 5 minutes, then stretch if desired.

Workout

Distance	1½ miles
Walking time	30 to 31 minutes
Pace	20- to 21-minute miles
Heart zone	60 to 69% max HR
Effort	RPE 2 to 3

Cool-down: Walk easily for 4 to 5 minutes, letting the front of your foot flap onto the ground to relax your shins, then stretch.

Calories used: 120

Comments: Maintain the slightly faster pace as suggested in workout 8 for an additional ¼ mile. If this is too much, try workout 5 or 8 again for several sessions.

Workout 10

Total time: 40 to 45 minutes

Warm-up: Walk easily for 5 to 7 minutes, then stretch if desired.

Workout

Distance	1½ miles
Walking time	27 to 30 minutes
Pace	18- to 20-minute miles
Heart zone	60 to 69% max HR
Effort	RPE 2 to 3

Cool-down: Walk easily for 5 minutes, rolling your shoulders back to stretch the front of your chest, then stretch.

Calories used: 125

Comments: This workout is the same distance as workout 9 but picks up the pace to edge your RPE toward 3. Try concentrating on the speed of your arm swing to get your feet moving. If you need to review the mechanics of an effective arm swing, take a look at chapter 2.

Workout 11

Total time: 45 to 55 minutes

Warm-up: Walk easily for 5 to 7 minutes, then stretch if desired.

Workout

Distance	1¾ miles
Walking time	32 to 35 minutes
Pace	18- to 20-minute miles
Heart zone	60 to 69% max HR
Effort	RPE 2 to 3

Cool-down: Walk easily for 5 minutes, rolling your shoulders back to stretch the front of your chest, then stretch.

Calories used: 145

Comments: This pace keeps you moving. Make sure you can complete this comfortably before trying a longer walk. If you need to drop back to workout 10, go ahead.

Workout 12

Total time: 50 to 55 minutes

Warm-up: Walk easily 5 to 7 minutes, then stretch if desired.

Workout

Distance	2 miles
Walking time	38 minutes
Pace	18- to 20-minute miles (see comments)
Heart zone	65 to 69% max HR
Effort	RPE 3

Terrain: Include a short, gradual hill in the second mile, if available.

Cool-down: Walk easily for 5 to 7 minutes, then stretch.

Calories used: 160 (180 with a slight incline)

Comments: Maintain the faster 18-minute-mile pace for the first mile, if possible, then allow yourself to finish the second mile at a 20-minute-mile pace, especially if you managed to find a slight incline or short hill. Don't worry if an incline significantly slows you down. It takes a whole new set of muscles and training to hike up hills. Just keep at it and do the best you can each time. Your cool-down is especially important after this workout; make sure you also take time to stretch.

CHAPTER 7

Medium and Steady Workouts

Your walks step up a notch in intensity with the medium and steady workouts in this chapter. Your perceived exertion is just a bit higher than in the short and easy workouts in chapter 6, values of 3 to 5, which correspond to 65 to 79 percent of your maximum heart rate (max HR). Before trying these slightly stepped-up workouts, make sure you are very comfortable with the easier workouts of 1½ to 2 miles. Note that the first two workouts in this chapter are of a slightly lower intensity than the others and could be considered introductory steady walks. Also feel free to mix these two lower-intensity workouts into your complete walking program.

So what is a steady walk compared to an easy one? These are still relatively easy walks, but you complete them without breaks and at a continuous pace. Find a speed you can maintain within the range and stride off the distance. The only challenge is holding a steady pace. *Speed* is not a concern, and you shouldn't equate steady with speedy. Still, even though speed is not important, if you can't maintain 20-minute miles (3 mph), you should consider sticking with easy workouts for a while to let your body and system build up to this steady pace.

These workouts are useful in several ways:

- Health walkers (beginners) looking for a spark of intensity once or twice a week can use these workouts to reach the next level.

- Health walkers (beginners) who intend to maintain a program of easy workouts can periodically include these workouts to add that bit of intensity as they work on building good health.
- Fitness walkers (intermediate) or athletic walkers (advanced) can include these workouts in a program of easy and steady workouts mixed with the other types of workouts listed in chapters 8 through 10.

The steady workouts increase to 4 miles compared to the easy workouts that maxed out at 2 miles. Again, they increase gradually, usually by only ¼ mile or ½ mile per workout. Your rate of perceived exertion (RPE), which is explained in chapter 4, remains moderate—mostly in the 3 to 4 range on the RPE scale of 0 to 10. An effort rating of 4 represents about 70 to 75 percent of your maximum heart rate (max HR); a 3 is 65 to 69 percent. The walking times in these workouts, not counting your warm-up and cool-down, is about 35 to 60 minutes.

Table 7.1 Preview: Medium and Steady Workouts

Workout	Distance (miles)	Total workout time (min)	Walking time (min)	Intensity (% max HR/RPE)
1	1¾	45-50	35-38	65-69/3
2	2	50-55	38	65-69/3
3	2	50-55	34-38	70-74/4
4	2¼	50-55	38-42	70-74/4
5	2¼	55-60	36-40	70-74/4
6	2½	50-55	37-38	70-74/4
7	3	60-70	45-54	70-74/4
8	3¼	60-70	49-56	70-74/4
9	3½	65-75	52-65	70-74/4
10	3¾	70-75	57-63	70-74/4
11	4	70-80	60-68	70-74/4
12	4¼	75-85	63-72	70-74/4

Workout 1

Total time: 45 to 50 minutes

Warm-up: Walk easily for 5 to 7 minutes, then stretch if desired.

Workout

Distance	1¾ miles
Walking time	35 to 38 minutes
Pace	18- to 20-minute miles
Heart zone	65 to 69% max HR
Effort	RPE 3

Cool-down: Walk easily for 5 to 7 minutes, then stretch.

Calories used: 140

Comments: Maintain the faster 18-minute-mile pace for the first mile, if possible, then allow yourself to finish the last ¾ of a mile at a more comfortable 20-minute-mile pace. Your cool-down will be extra important; make sure you also take time to stretch.

Workout 2

Total time: 50 to 55 minutes

Warm-up: Walk easily for 5 to 7 minutes, then stretch if desired.

Workout

Distance	2 miles
Walking time	38 minutes
Pace	18- to 20-minute miles (see comments)
Heart zone	65 to 69% max HR
Effort	RPE 3

Cool-down: Walk easily for 5 to 7 minutes, then stretch.

Calories used: 160

Comments: In this workout, try the opposite of the first one: Start out at a 20-minute-mile pace for the first mile, then pick it up to an 18-minute-mile pace in the second. This is tougher than slowing down at the end, so be sure you can accomplish workout 1 before trying this challenge.

Workout 3

Total time: 50 to 55 minutes

Warm-up: Walk for 4 to 5 minutes at a pace slightly slower than your pace for the workout, then stretch if desired.

Workout

Distance	2 miles
Walking time	34 to 38 minutes
Pace	17- to 19-minute miles
Heart zone	70 to 74% max HR
Effort	RPE 4

Cool-down: Walk easily for 5 minutes, then stretch.

Calories used: 170

Comments: Start with an 18- or even 19-minute-mile pace, speed up to 17- or 18-minute miles if you can handle the pace without overdoing it, then slow to 18- to 19-minute miles. The transitions should be relatively smooth, without noticeable bursts. Don't feel compelled to hit a very brisk 15-minute-mile pace. The speedy workouts are in chapter 9, so quickness is not the intent here.

Workout 4

Total time: 50 to 55 minutes

Warm-up: Walk for 4 to 5 minutes at a pace slightly slower than your pace for the workout, then stretch if desired.

Workout

Distance	2¼ miles
Walking time	38 to 42 minutes
Pace	17- to 19-minute miles
Heart zone	70 to 74% max HR
Effort	RPE 4

Cool-down: Walk easily for 5 minutes, then stretch.

Calories used: 190

Comments: This workout is steady, but comfortable, with a very moderate perceived effort. This workout provides a great opportunity to concentrate on a specific part of your technique, such as arm swing.

Workout 5

Total time: 55 to 60 minutes

Warm-up: Walk for 4 to 5 minutes slightly slower than your pace for the workout, then stretch if desired.

Workout

Distance	2¼ miles
Walking time	36 to 40 minutes
Pace	16- to 18-minute miles
Heart zone	70 to 74% max HR
Effort	RPE 4

Cool-down: Walk easily for 5 minutes, then stretch.

Calories used: 190

Comments: In this fifth steady workout, check to see if you can maintain a slightly faster steady pace than you thought you could or have tried in the previous walks. For fun, include a slight hill or incline—even a driveway or other ramp—and focus on pushing off of the tip of your foot. This technique is easier to feel on an incline because you have to use a significant push to get yourself up the hill.

Workout 6

Total time: 50 to 55 minutes

Warm-up: Walk for 5 to 7 minutes at a pace slower than your goal pace for the day, or walk the first half mile of the workout at a slower pace. Stretch if desired.

Workout

Distance	2½ miles
Walking time	37 to 38 minutes
Pace	16- to 18-minute miles
Heart zone	70 to 74% max HR
Effort	RPE 4

Cool-down: Walk easily for 5 to 7 minutes, then stretch.

Calories used: 230

Comments: This workout is just a ¼ mile (or 4 to 5 minutes) longer than previous workouts. If you can maintain the same pace, go for it, but it should still feel comfortable. You've spent one workout focusing on arms and another on push-off; use this one to practice keeping your abdominals tight and your hips pulled under you so that you are standing tall.

Workout 7

Total time: 60 to 70 minutes

Warm-up: Walk for 5 to 7 minutes at a pace slower than your goal pace for the day, or walk the first ½ mile of the workout at a slower pace. Stretch if desired.

Workout

Distance	3 miles
Walking time	45 to 54 minutes
Pace	15- to 18-minute miles
Heart zone	70 to 74% max HR
Effort	RPE 4

Cool-down: Walk easily for 5 to 7 minutes, then stretch.

Calories used: 275

Comments: A 15-minute mile may sound fast, but it's used as the true definition of a "brisk" walk. However, if it's so brisk that you exceed an RPE of 4, taper back to a slower pace. Repeat this workout a few times as you begin experimenting with 15-minute miles. Because 3 miles usually take 45 minutes to an hour, this can become a standard workout, and one you may find that you come back to frequently.

Workout 8

Total time: 60 to 70 minutes

Warm-up: Walk for 5 to 7 minutes at a pace slower than your goal pace for the day, or walk the first ½ mile of the workout at a slower pace. Stretch if desired.

Workout

Distance	3¼ miles
Walking time	49 to 56 minutes
Pace	15- to 18-minute miles
Heart zone	70 to 74% max HR
Effort	RPE 4

Cool-down: Walk easily for 5 to 7 minutes, then stretch.

Calories used: 300

Comments: This workout adds ¼ mile in a typical progression to help you gain confidence and strength. Nevertheless, once you can master this distance at a moderate and steady pace, it could also become a staple workout for building a base of fitness and health. Try to hit edgier mile times faster than 18 minutes so you can work your way to hitting the 15-minute mile.

Workout 9

Total time: 65 to 75 minutes

Warm-up: Walk for about 5 to 7 minutes at a pace slower than your goal pace, relaxing your shoulders and visualizing your success at this first longer walk. Stretch if desired.

Workout

Distance	3½ miles
Walking time	52 to 65 minutes
Pace	15- to 18-minute miles
Heart zone	70 to 74% max HR
Effort	RPE 4

Cool-down: Walk easily for 5 to 7 minutes, then stretch.

Calories used: 315

Comments: Don't push yourself to go too fast, especially in the beginning when you feel fresh and it's tempting to stride faster than your steady pace. The goal is to finish feeling energized.

Workout 10

Total time: 70 to 75 minutes

Warm-up: Walk for about 5 to 7 minutes at a pace slower than your goal pace, relaxing your shoulders. Stretch if desired.

Workout

Distance	3¾ miles
Walking time	57 to 63 minutes
Pace	15- to 17-minute miles
Heart zone	70 to 74% max HR
Effort	RPE 4

Cool-down: Walk easily for 5 to 7 minutes, then stretch.

Calories used: 340

Comments: This workout is close enough to 4 miles that some consider it a long walk. Be careful with it; don't increase distance or speed until you're comfortable with the first steady workouts. During this workout start out at a faster pace, then let yourself slow in the last half. Remember, the push-off with the toe of the back foot should remain strong, even on flat terrain—you practiced it earlier.

Workout 11

Total time: 70 to 80 minutes

Warm-up: Walk for 5 to 7 minutes at a pace slower than your goal pace, sensing the rolling motion in your feet. Stretch if desired.

Workout

Distance	4 miles
Walking time	60 to 68 minutes
Pace	15- to 17-minute miles
Heart zone	70 to 74% max HR
Effort	RPE 4

Cool-down: Walk easily for 5 to 7 minutes, then stretch.

Calories used: 360

Comments: Tackle this workout with the intention of completing the entire distance at a steady clip. With workouts creeping toward an hour and perhaps beyond it depending on your pace, you might want to find a friend to walk with. Once you get in a zone, you'll find that an hour zips by, especially if you find a new park or neighborhood to explore.

Workout 12

Total time: 75 to 85 minutes

Warm-up: Walk for about 5 to 7 minutes at a pace slower than your goal pace, sensing the rolling motion in your feet from heel to toe. Stretch if desired.

Workout

Distance	4¼ miles
Walking time	63 to 72 minutes
Pace	15- to 17-minute miles
Heart zone	70 to 74% max HR
Effort	RPE 4

Cool-down: Walk easily for 5 to 7 minutes, then stretch.

Calories used: 390

Comments: This workout pushes your steady walks past the 4-mile mark. Because you are investing more than an hour, this might seem like a long workout. Therefore, use it sparingly and adapt it as a long walk, based on the descriptions and instruction in chapter 10, if it seems appropriate.

8

Medium and Quicker Workouts

Quicker workouts are intended for walkers at the advanced health walker or intermediate fitness walker level or higher. That's because these workouts ask you to push the envelope just a bit, moving beyond comfortable to what some call comfortably hard. Although this might sound like a contradiction, it isn't. Comfortable is just that: easy, with no thought needed to continue at that pace. On the other hand, hard is highly demanding and suitable only for advanced athletic exercisers because of the effort and heart rate levels reached. Normally, you must focus to maintain a hard pace. But a *comfortably hard* pace is not terribly difficult to reach; however, you might have to focus slightly to maintain it without slipping back to an easy pace.

The pace for medium and quicker workouts should allow you to converse without becoming breathless, but you will feel your breathing and heart rates increase a notch more than with steady workouts. Depending on how hard you make the effort within the range of comfortable, you could do several of these workouts a week. They are not, however, everyday workouts.

Medium and quicker workouts are useful for the following:

- Beginner health walkers, but not true novices or those new to exercise, look for a brisk and upbeat pace to challenge their cardiovascular fitness, additional muscular toning, and caloric use. These can be used once a week, usually as part of a schedule of three workouts a week.

- Intermediate fitness walkers who can step up to this up-tempo challenge can use these workouts twice a week or so as part of a schedule of four or five workouts a week.
- Advanced athletic walkers who need a brisk change of pace sprinkled into a week of easy, long, speedy, and steady workouts can add one of these workouts once or twice a week as part of an advanced schedule of five or six workouts a week.

As in the other chapters, the workouts in this section step up gradually in mileage so that you can progress as needed throughout the range offered, which in this case is 1½ to 4 miles. Your rate of perceived exertion (RPE) steps up a notch, hitting 4 to 6 on a scale of 0 to 10. These values correspond to a maximum heart rate (max HR) of 70 to 84 percent. These workouts may not be appreciably longer than the steady workouts because you're covering similar distances but at a faster pace. So look for walking times of about 25 to 50 minutes. Once you add in your warm-up, cool-down and postworkout stretch, your workout time could hit 40 to 65 minutes.

The last two workouts introduce quick walks that incorporate a form of interval training but not the speed intervals outlined in chapter 9. Instead, these workouts include longer distances that you repeat two or three times, depending on the distance, with short rests between them. These interval-type quick walks are intended for intermediate and advanced walkers looking for more challenge.

Workouts 9 and 10 are best done at weekend fun run 5-kilometer (3.1-mile) events. Participation in these events can boost your pace because of the excitement of the crowd. Who doesn't get fired up by a little competition? Add these four workouts as you become comfortable with a more challenging pace.

Table 8.1 Preview: Medium and Quicker Workouts

Workout	Distance (miles)	Total workout time (min)	Walking time (min)	Intensity (% max HR/RPE)
1	1½	40	23-24	70-79/4
2	2	40-45	30-31	70-79/4-5
3	2¼	45-50	34	70-79/4-5
4	2½	50-55	37-38	70-79/4-5
5	3	55-65	45-46	70-79/4-5
6	2	45-50	29	75-79/5
7	2	45-50	28	75-84/5-6
8	2½	50-55	33-35	75-84/5-6
9	3.1	55-60	43-44	80-84/6
10	3.1	55-60	40-42	80-84/6
11	4	70-75	52	80-84/6
12	4	70-75	52	80-84/6

Workout 1

Total time: 40 minutes

Warm-up: Walk for 5 to 7 minutes at a pace slightly slower than your steady walk pace, then stretch if desired.

Workout

Distance	1½ miles
Walking time	23 to 24 minutes
Pace	15- to 16-minute miles
Heart zone	70 to 79% max HR
Effort	RPE 4

Cool-down: Walk easily for 5 to 7 minutes, then stretch.

Calories used: 130

Comments: As you tackle this workout, think fast feet and powerful arms to keep you going at 15- to 16-minute miles. If you can't hold a faster pace while maintaining an RPE of about 4, try a few more of the slower paced steady walks. Above all else, these quick walks should not leave you breathless—breathing hard, yes, but not feeling out of breath.

Workout 2

Total time: 40 to 45 minutes

Warm-up: Walk for 5 to 7 minutes at a pace slightly slower than your steady walk pace, then stretch if desired.

Workout

Distance	2 miles
Walking time	30 to 31 minutes
Pace	15- to 16-minute miles
Heart zone	70 to 79% max HR
Effort	RPE 4 to 5

Cool-down: Walk easily for 5 to 7 minutes, then stretch.

Calories used: 170 (210 with gradual incline; see comments)

Comments: Keep your shoulders relaxed as you tackle this workout at a 15-minute-mile pace. If you can, throw hills into the last mile of your route. Expect to slow slightly on the incline—perhaps to 16-minute miles—but don't stroll too easily. Practice your rear push-off as you stride uphill, and be sure to keep your abdominals tight and avoid leaning forward from your waist.

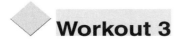

Workout 3

Total time: 45 to 50 minutes

Warm-up: Walk for 5 to 7 minutes at a pace slightly slower than your steady walk pace, then stretch if desired.

Workout

Distance	2¼ miles
Walking time	34 minutes
Pace	15-minute miles
Heart zone	70 to 79% max HR
Effort	RPE 4 to 5

Cool-down: Walk easily for 5 to 7 minutes, then stretch.

Calories used: 195

Comments: You should be able to maintain 15-minute miles for this workout. If not, tackle the shorter workouts 1 and 2 until you are confident that you can maintain the pace.

Workout 4

Total time: 50 to 55 minutes

Warm-up: Walk for 5 to 7 minutes at a pace slower than your goal pace for the day, or walk the first ½ mile of the workout slower. Stretch if desired.

Workout

Distance	2½ miles
Walking time	37 to 38 minutes
Pace	15-minute miles
Heart zone	70 to 79% max HR
Effort	RPE 4 to 5

Cool-down: Walk easily for 5 to 7 minutes, then stretch.

Calories used: 235

Comments: Think about moving your feet quickly to keep the pace. Your goal is to stick closer to 15-minute miles, although slowing the pace slightly in the last ½ mile will help you finish.

Workout 5

Total time: 55 to 65 minutes

Warm-up: Walk for 5 to 7 minutes at a pace slower than your goal pace for the day, or walk the first ½ mile of the workout slower. Stretch if desired.

Workout

Distance	3 miles
Walking time	45 to 46 minutes
Pace	15-minute miles
Heart zone	70 to 79% max HR
Effort	RPE 4 to 5

Cool-down: Walk easily for 5 to 7 minutes, then stretch.

Calories used: 280 (350 with some gradual hills)

Comments: Aim for a brisk 15-minute pace, but if you incorporate minor inclines, remember that your pace will slow slightly. Lean into the hill from your ankles not your waist, and use the incline to concentrate on a powerful toe push-off. If you're ready to try increasing your speed to slightly quicker than 15-minute miles, give it a whirl for a couple of minutes here and there, and be comfortable knowing your RPE will likely be a strong 5. This attempt will prime you for quicker workouts.

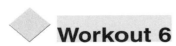

Workout 6

Total time: 45 to 50 minutes

Warm-up: Walk for about 5 minutes at a slow pace, stretch, then walk for another 2 to 3 minutes at a more moderate pace, picking it up even faster for the last minute. Finish your warm-up right before the start.

Workout

Distance	2 miles
Walking time	29 minutes
Pace	First mile, steady 15-minute mile; second mile, 14-minute mile
Heart zone	75 to 79% max HR
Effort	RPE 5

Cool-down: Walk easily for 5 to 7 minutes, then stretch.

Calories used: 195

Comments: By now you may have found a bike path nearby with measured miles, or you've clocked a stretch of road near your home or in the local park. Use those routes for a quick 2 miles. Or pick a weekend fun run with a 2-mile walk segment. After your warm-up, take a few deep breaths to relax, and focus on starting out at your brisk pace without getting all revved up and starting too fast. Use the pent-up energy to put the hammer down for the second mile, but don't push the pace to the point that you're out of breath.

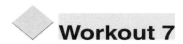

Workout 7

Total time: 45 to 50 minutes

Warm-up: Walk for about 5 minutes at a slow pace, stretch, then walk for another 2 to 3 minutes at a more moderate pace, picking it up even faster for the last minute. Finish your warm-up right before the start.

Workout

Distance	2 miles
Walking time	28 minutes
Pace	14-minute miles
Heart zone	75 to 84% max HR
Effort	RPE 5 to 6

Cool-down: Walk easily for 5 to 7 minutes, then stretch.

Calories used: 200 (250 with rolling hills)

Comments: Use the same route you used for workout 6, the measured path or street. Or choose another weekend event a few weeks later. Now that you've practiced, your goal is to go out at a quick pace—briskly steady and comfortably hard—and maintain it. For an extra challenge, try this on a route with slightly rolling hills.

Workout 8

Total time: 50 to 55 minutes

Warm-up: Walk for about 5 minutes at a slow pace, stretch, then walk for another 2 minutes at a more moderate pace.

Workout

Distance	2½ miles
Walking time	33 to 35 minutes
Pace	13- to 14-minute miles
Heart zone	75 to 84% max HR
Effort	RPE 5 to 6

Cool-down: Walk easily for 5 to 7 minutes, then stretch.

Calories used: 290

Comments: This is great preparation for the next four workouts (two 5-kilometer races and the more intense quick intervals). You can invent lots of variations. Try maintaining 14-minute miles, or start at 13-minute-mile pace and finish at 14, or start at 14 and pump up the finish to 13, or even try to maintain 13-minute miles when you're ready. Now that's brisk and quick!

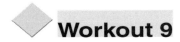

Workout 9

Total time: 55 to 60 minutes

Warm-up: Walk for about 5 minutes at a slow pace, stretch, then walk for another 2 to 3 minutes at a more moderate pace, picking it up even faster for the last minute. Finish your warm-up right before the start.

Workout

Distance	3.1 miles (5 kilometers)
Walking time	43 to 44 minutes
Pace	14-minute miles
Heart zone	80 to 84% max HR
Effort	RPE 6

Cool-down: Walk easily for 5 to 7 minutes, then stretch.

Calories used: 285 (350 with rolling hills)

Comments: Stick to about 14-minute miles, a good pace for your first 5-kilometer event, especially if it is over rolling hills. If you feel like it, pick up your speed in the last ½ mile. I bet you'll beat some joggers! Don't neglect the cool-down, which is absolutely necessary after more intense workouts. The beauty of these quicker workouts is that each primes you for the next, and they can be mixed and matched at different speeds. For example, you can use workout 8 to prepare yourself for this one, then go back and do workout 8 a few times at a faster clip to prime yourself for workout 10!

Workout 10

Total time: 55 to 60 minutes

Warm-up: Walk for about 5 minutes at a slow pace, stretch, then walk for another 2 to 3 minutes at a more moderate pace, picking it up even faster for the last minute. Finish your warm-up right before the start.

Workout

Distance	3.1 miles (5 kilometers)
Walking time	40 to 42 minutes
Pace	13-minute miles
Heart zone	80 to 84% max HR
Effort	RPE 6

Cool-down: Walk easily for 5 to 7 minutes, then stretch.

Calories used: 310

Comments: Be sure to repeat workouts 6 through 8 before moving on to this quicker-tempo workout. As in workout 9, find a local 5-kilometer run, but enter the run, not the walk. The energy of the pack will help keep you going. Pick one with markers at every mile and someone calling out times (split times). That'll help you keep your pace. Don't start out too fast. And don't worry about being last. You'll be surprised how slowly some joggers run. Occasionally doing 5-kilometer fun runs can also be a great way to assess how far your fitness has come based on the speed and intensity you can now accomplish. One warning: Don't get frustrated if a course seems long. Unless a racecourse is certified (i.e., measured and proved accurate by an overseeing association), it may not be accurate and could be short or long.

Workout 11

Total time: 70 to 75 minutes

Warm-up: Walk about a mile at an easy pace, stretch, then walk for another 3 to 4 minutes at a more moderate pace. Pick up the speed in the last minute to a sprint pace. Let your heart rate drop to the easy-pace level before starting.

Workout

Distance	4 miles
Walking time	52 minutes
Pace	13-minute miles for the "quick" intervals
Heart zone	80 to 84% max HR
Effort	RPE 6

Cool-down: Walk easily for ½ mile to a mile, then stretch.

Calories used: 420

Comments: This workout consists of three intervals, all designed to hone your quick pace. All are separated by a short rest interval. The first segment is 2 miles, the second and third are each 1 mile. Now that you're ready to push it, try to keep your pace at 13-minute miles. As you progress, you can try to drop it a bit if you'd like, which may raise your RPE too. After the first interval, rest 5 or 6 minutes by walking around easily, even 16-minute miles or slower, so that your heart and breathing rate drop. After the second interval, rest by strolling 2 or 3 minutes. Perceived exertion and heart rate during the strolling rest should drop to equal your early warm-up levels. An active cool-down, where you continue to walk easily, is vital after an intense workout to offset muscle soreness.

Workout 12

Total time: 70 to 75 minutes

Warm-up: Walk about a mile at an easy pace, stretch, then walk for another 3 to 4 minutes at a more moderate pace. Pick up the speed in the last minute to a sprint pace. Let your heart rate drop to the easy-pace level before starting.

Workout

Distance	4 miles
Walking time	52 minutes
Pace	13-minute miles for the "quick" intervals
Heart zone	80 to 84% max HR
Effort	RPE 6

Cool-down: Walk easily for ½ mile to a mile, then stretch.

Calories used: 420

Comments: This workout is similar to workout 11, but consists of two 2-mile intervals. After the first 2-mile interval take about a 7- to 8-minute rest while strolling around easily, then do another 2-mile interval at the same pace.

CHAPTER **9**

Short and Fast Workouts

You may sometimes hear short and fast workouts called speed play. As the name implies, you get to tinker, or play, with speedier bursts of walking. Similar to the disciplined interval workouts on the track, speed play is a less structured style that uses the natural terrain and environment. These workouts should challenge your technique and personal speed, yet remain fun and playful. They are suitable for intermediate to advanced fitness and athletic walkers—someone whose primary form of exercise is walking or someone who is fit enough to undertake challenging athletic walking workouts a couple of times a week. Try these workouts only if you've been walking for fitness for many months or even years. These speedy interval-like walks are not suitable for health-oriented beginning exercisers or for novice walkers, but of course everyone can work up to them. An advanced health (beginning) walker may try the first two workouts, but if you become overly breathless or fatigued, slow down or take longer rests.

Short and fast walks can serve several purposes:

- Intermediate-level fitness walkers can use these workouts once a week or so to add a little zip to their routine and to teach their legs how to move faster. Because they build aerobic fitness and muscle endurance, slower walks will seem easier after this type of workout.

- Advanced athletic types and those who try to "race" during their workouts or who get serious at the starting line of a weekend fun run can use these workouts to give them an extra push. These workouts can be included weekly, but no more than twice in one week.

Use these workouts carefully. They are too high in intensity to be done every day. But, because they are short (none longer than about 45 minutes and most around 30), they are easier to squeeze in after a long day at work or during a long lunch break.

These short and fast workouts, like the others, are listed in order of increasing mileage or intensity or both. The workout distances, not including the warm-up or cool down, aren't terribly long because the workouts are of higher intensity. These workouts cover 1½ to 3 miles. Because of the intensity, your rating of perceived exertion (RPE) and corresponding heart rates will be higher than in previous chapters. Your RPE should reach 5 to 7 on average during a workout, or 75 to 89 percent of your maximum heart rate (max HR). Because of this increased intensity, it is especially important to listen to your body to avoid overexertion that could lead to injury or strain. Always listen and pay attention: If your body says something hurts or doesn't feel good, slow down or stop. The actual workouts will last only 23 to 42 minutes. Adding a warm-up, cool-down, and postworkout stretching, your workout time could hit 35 to 60 minutes.

Recovery, the rest interval between fast bouts of walking, must be taken seriously during these workouts. The last two workouts of chapter 8 introduced this concept, but in short and fast workouts, it becomes very important. During a recovery you walk slowly to allow your heart and breathing rates to return to the same levels as in the medium and steady workouts from chapter 7. This could be an RPE as low as 3. You will discover that as you get more aerobically fit, your heart and breathing rates decrease more quickly.

In these workouts the warm-ups increase in length and the intensity increases gradually, although you still start at a very easy pace. These longer and more specific warm-ups prepare your body for intense workouts by warming it up to nearly that level.

Table 9.1   Preview: Short and Fast Workouts

Workout	Distance (miles)	Total workout time (min)	Walking time (min)	Intensity (% max HR/RPE)
1	1½	35-40	24-26	75-79/5 (avg)
2	1½	35-40	23-25	75-79/5 (avg)
3	2	40-45	30-32	75-79/5 (avg)
4	2	40-45	30-32	75-79/5 (avg)
5	2½	50-55	35-36	75-79/5 (avg)
6	3	55-60	41-42	75-79/5 (avg)
7	2	40-45	26-28	75-79/5 (avg)
8	2½	45-50	32-35	80-84/6 (avg)
9	2½	45-50	32-35	80-84/6 (avg)
10	3	55-60	40-42	85-89/7 (avg)
11	3	50-55	36-39	85-89/7 (avg)
12	3	50-55	36-39	85-89/7 (avg)

Workout 1

Total time: 35 to 40 minutes

Warm-up: Walk for about 5 minutes at a pace slightly slower than your steady pace, followed by another minute at your steady pace, then stretch.

Workout

Distance	1½ miles
Walking time	24 to 26 minutes
Pace	16- to 17-minute miles, with 15-second medium-hard bursts of 14- to 15-minute miles every 5 minutes
Heart zone	75 to 79% max HR
Effort	RPE 5 (average)

Cool-down: Walk easily for 5 to 7 minutes, then stretch.

Calories used: 135

Comments: The end of the warm-up is a little quicker to prepare your body for the speed play to come. Try only very short bursts the first time and allow yourself to recover with a slower but still steady pace between the bursts. As you experiment with this kind of speedier walking, feel free to do fewer intervals or take longer rests.

Workout 2

Total time: 35 to 40 minutes

Warm-up: Walk for about 5 minutes at a pace slightly slower than your steady pace, followed by another minute at your steady pace, then stretch.

Workout

Distance	1½ miles
Walking time	23 to 25 minutes
Pace	16- to 17-minute miles, with 30-second medium-hard bursts of 14- to 15-minute miles every 4 to 5 minutes
Heart zone	75 to 79% max HR
Effort	RPE 5 (average)

Cool-down: Walk easily for 5 to 7 minutes, then stretch.

Calories used: 135

Comments: Lengthen the speedier bursts slightly, but keep the recovery intervals between them at your steady pace. Think about strong feet grabbing the ground in front of you and pulling it beneath and behind you during the speedier sections. The recoveries can range from 4 to 5 minutes. If you're up to it, use the shorter range.

Workout 3

Total time: 40 to 45 minutes

Warm-up: Walk for about 5 minutes at a pace slightly slower than your steady pace, followed by another minute at your steady pace, then stretch.

Workout	
Distance	2 miles
Walking time	30 to 32 minutes
Pace	16- to 17-minute miles, with 1-minute bursts of 14- to 15-minute miles every 4 to 5 minutes
Heart zone	75 to 79% max HR
Effort	RPE 5 (average)

Cool-down: Walk easily for 5 to 7 minutes, then stretch.

Calories used: 170

Comments: Make sure you're comfortable with the 30-second speedy intervals in workout 2 before graduating to 1-minute bursts. Your goal is to keep the walking pace between the fast bursts slightly more up-tempo, but still allowing recovery so that you can go fast again.

Workout 4

Total time: 40 to 45 minutes

Warm-up: Walk for about 5 minutes at a pace slightly slower than your steady pace, followed by another minute at your steady pace, then stretch.

Workout

Distance	2 miles
Walking time	30 to 32 minutes
Pace	16- to 17-minute miles, with 30-second bursts of 14- to 15-minute miles every 3 to 4 minutes
Heart zone	75 to 79% max HR
Effort	RPE 5 (average)

Cool-down: Walk easily for 5 to 7 minutes, then stretch.

Calories used: 170

Comments: You will probably be able to fit in six or seven speedy intervals during your 2 miles. Once again, you're challenged to shorten the recovery just a bit between the speedy sections. If this workout is too intense, just take more time getting comfortable with workouts 2 and 3 before trying this.

Workout 5

Total time: 50 to 55 minutes

Warm-up: Walk for 5 to 7 minutes at a pace slower than your 15-minute-mile pace, picking up the pace slightly toward the end, then stretch.

Workout

Distance	2½ miles
Walking time	35 to 36 minutes
Pace	16-minute miles, with 1-minute bursts of 14-minute miles every 3 to 5 minutes
Heart zone	75 to 79% max HR
Effort	RPE 5 (average)

Cool-down: Walk easily for 5 to 7 minutes, then stretch.

Calories used: 235

Comments: This workout lets you push your recovery a little by taking only 3 minutes between speedier segments. You can work up to the shorter recovery by taking 5 minutes one week, 4 the next, and 3 the next week. Or you can step down the recoveries in one workout, for example, doing your first one or two with 5 minutes, then a couple with 4, then whatever you have left with 3 minutes between.

Workout 6

Total time: 55 to 60 minutes

Warm-up: Walk for 5 to 7 minutes at a pace slower than your 15-minute-mile pace, picking up the pace slightly toward the end, then stretch.

Workout

Distance	3 miles
Walking time	41 to 42 minutes
Pace	15-minute miles, with 1-minute bursts of 14-minute miles every 4 to 5 minutes
Heart zone	75 to 79% max HR
Effort	RPE 5 (average)

Cool-down: Walk easily for 5 to 7 minutes, then stretch.

Calories used: 285

Comments: Here it comes: the prod not only to hold 15-minutes miles but also the extra push to make your speedier segments even speedier. This may require focus, but as you become more fit, you'll wonder why it seemed so hard before. When that happens, increase the speed of the speedy sections and recovery intervals for more of a challenge.

Workout 7

Total time: 40 to 45 minutes

Warm-up: Walk for 5 minutes at a slow pace, stretch, then walk another 2 minutes at a more moderate pace, picking it up even faster for your final 30 seconds.

Workout

Distance	2 miles
Walking time	26 to 28 minutes
Pace	14- to 15-minute miles, with 2-minute bursts close to 13-minute miles, followed by 6 minutes at the slower pace
Heart zone	75 to 79% max HR
Effort	RPE 5 (average)

Cool-down: Walk easily for 5 to 7 minutes, then stretch.

Calories used: 190

Comments: This workout drops back in distance because both the pace and length of the fast segments are stepped up. Although you get a little more recovery, this workout is very challenging. Be sure to monitor your perceived exertion and heart rate. Both should be at the bottom end of their given ranges before your next burst. If not, take another minute or so to recover. If your perceived exertion and heart rates reach the lower end more quickly, try shortening the recovery period.

Workout 8

Total time: 45 to 50 minutes

Warm-up: Walk for about 5 minutes at a slow pace, stretch, then walk for another 2 minutes at a more moderate pace, picking it up even faster for the last 30 seconds.

Workout	
Distance	2½ miles
Walking time	32 to 35 minutes
Pace	13- to 15-minute miles, with 3-minute bursts close to 13-minute miles, alternating with 7 minutes at the slower pace
Heart zone	80 to 84% max HR
Effort	RPE 6 (average)

Cool-down: Walk easily for 5 to 7 minutes, then stretch.

Calories used: 240

Comments: Concentrate on moving your arms and feet quickly to propel yourself forward. Go back to workout 7 (or even a couple before that) if your heart rate doesn't drop about 10 beats per minute in recovery. A 3-minute speed segment will seem long the first time you try it, but once you get used to it, you'll hit a flow. You could try these on a track if you'd like and change the speedy part to one lap. You'll be surprised at how fast you can go. If you do this workout on a track, however, move to the outside lanes when you are recovering and walking slowly.

Workout 9

Total time: 45 to 50 minutes

Warm-up: Walk for about 5 minutes at a slow pace, stretch, then walk for another 2 minutes at a more moderate pace, picking it up even faster for the last 30 seconds.

Workout

Distance	2½ miles
Walking time	32 to 35 minutes
Pace	13- to 15-minute miles, with 3-minute bursts close to 13-minute miles, alternating with 7 minutes at the slower pace
Heart zone	80 to 84% max HR
Effort	RPE 6 (average)

Cool-down: Walk easily for 5 to 7 minutes, then stretch.

Calories used: 265

Comments: This workout is the same length and done at the same pace as workout 8, but you incorporate gradual hills into the speedy bursts. Push yourself up the hills by leaning into the incline from your ankles and using your arm and back muscles to power your arm swing, as well as the power of the toe push from the back foot. If you walk in a multilevel mall, use the stairs to achieve the intensity bursts.

Workout 10

Total time: 55 to 60 minutes

Warm-up: Walk for about 5 minutes at a slow pace, stretch, then walk for another 2 minutes at a more moderate pace, picking it up even faster for the last 30 seconds.

Workout

Distance	3 miles
Walking time	40 to 42 minutes
Pace	13- to 14-minute miles, with 4-minute bursts no slower than 13-minute miles, alternating with 8 minutes at the slower but still steady pace
Heart zone	85 to 89% max HR
Effort	RPE 7 (average)

Cool-down: Walk easily for 5 to 7 minutes, then stretch.

Calories used: 295

Comments: Use the easy but steady recovery pace to give you the strength to push hard during the speed play. Experiment with shorter recovery periods as you become more fit and your perceived exertion and heart rates drop more quickly. If you'd like to try these on a track, do about one and a half laps for the speedy part.

Workout 11

Total time: 50 to 55 minutes

Warm-up: Walk for about 5 minutes at a slow pace, stretch, then walk for another 2 minutes at a more moderate pace, picking it up even faster for the last 30 seconds.

Workout

Distance	3 miles
Walking time	36 to 39 minutes
Pace	Close to 13-minute miles, with 40-second to 1-minute segments nearly as hard as you can. Allow 3 to 4 minutes of recovery after each burst.
Heart zone	85 to 89% max HR
Effort	RPE 7 (average)

Cool-down: Walk easily for 5 to 7 minutes, then stretch.

Calories used: 300

Comments: Be careful on the 1-minute sprints. Be sure you can maintain this pace for the entire minute. These are fast but certainly not all out. During the 3- to 4-minute recovery breaks, try not to let the pace drop lower than about 14- to 15-minute miles. Your heart rate will drop only a few beats. This workout is for intermediate fitness to advanced athletic walkers.

Workout 12

Total time: 50 to 55 minutes

Warm-up: Walk for about 5 minutes at a pace slightly slower than your steady pace, another minute at your steady pace, then stretch.

Workout

Distance	3 miles
Walking time	36 to 39 minutes
Pace	14- to 15-minute miles, with 1-minute bursts of 13-minute miles every 2 minutes
Heart zone	85 to 89% max HR
Effort	RPE 7 (average)

Cool-down: Walk easily for 5 to 7 minutes, then stretch.

Calories used: 290

Comments: Make sure you're comfortable with workouts with 30-second speedy intervals before graduating to 1-minute bursts with only 2 minutes to recover. Your goal is to keep the walk between bursts slightly up-tempo. If you find yourself dragging, then tackle workout 11 a few more times. Once this workout is comfortably hard and not too hard, it is a great workout to toss into your walking program frequently.

CHAPTER 10

Long and Steady Workouts

Although these long and steady walks are described in the last of the five chapters of workouts, that doesn't imply that they are only for advanced athletic walkers or are the most difficult workouts. Long workouts are a vital part of virtually any walking program if the length is appropriate for the walker's level—the definition of long can vary widely. The body gets used to trudging along at one pace for 3 miles three times a week, 6 miles four times a week, or whatever you do for your level and ability. If you don't push it once or twice a week—say, a speedy workout from chapter 9 or a long workout—your body gets set in its ways. The long workouts, like the speedy short ones, force your body out of its comfort zone. And if done once every week or two, they can provide an amazing amount of strength.

You should be able to complete a long and steady workout at a steady pace without stopping, except for breaks to refuel, rehydrate, and stretch. The pace should be comfortable, allowing you to talk to a friend or just enjoy the passing scenery. With the work week often crammed and busy, weekends can be a great time to treat yourself to extra time for a long workout.

The workouts in this chapter range from 3 to 13.1 miles. Your rate of perceived exertion (RPE) will typically be about 4 to 6 on the RPE scale of 1 to 10. This corresponds to 70 to 84 percent of maximum heart rate (max HR). I've thrown in a couple of challenge workouts that ask you to jump into weekend fun runs of various distances, including 10 kilometers (6.2 miles). Depending on your goal, you can either jump into the race and walk your normal long workout at an effort level of 4 to 6, enjoying the company and aid stations, or you can push the pace a bit, upping your effort level to as much as 7 or 8 (85 to 94 percent max HR). In this case, your perceived exertion may vary widely between warm-up and the first part of the race, the middle, and the final push—ranging from perhaps 5 to 8. However, only intermediate or more experienced walkers have strengthened their heart muscle enough to try pushing into the 7 to 8 effort level.

Defining *Long*

No walker, no matter what level (except the true health-oriented beginner), should shy away from the rather intimidating word *long*. For some, 2 miles is long. For others, 10 or 12 miles might be long. It doesn't matter! Just do what's long for you and you'll gain you'll grow stronger.

A long workout should be slightly longer in both time and distance than your normal workouts. One rule of thumb is to make them about 25 to 35 percent of your total mileage for the week. For example, if you walk four 2-mile workouts each week, your long workout might only be 2½ or 3 miles. If you do five 5-mile walks each week, your long workout could be 7½ or 8 miles. But don't feel bound by that formula. If you normally walk three times a week, 3 miles each time, a long workout will likely be 3½ or 4 miles even though that doesn't quite follow the formula. If you are an advanced walker who puts in 30 to 35 miles a week (perhaps averaging 7 miles each time), you may be more comfortable with a long workout of 9 miles rather than the 10 or more the calculation tells you to do. The bottom line is: Use your head.

Because the definition of long varies greatly, a long workout could last anywhere from 50 minutes to more than 2½ hours. And remember, once your workout gets up to 75 minutes, you must take in small amounts of carbohydrates to fuel your engine so you don't hit the wall. You must also drink water during any walk over an hour. This is addressed briefly in chapter 3.

You should now be able to manage the typical 15-minute-mile pace commonly known as a brisk walk. All these long workouts use that pace as a benchmark, with encouragement to push it to 13s or 14s on a few. However, if you need to, walk at a 16- or 17-minutes-per-mile pace instead. Or if you're really pumping up the speed and can push 12- or 13-minute miles, nobody is holding you back!

Table 10.1 Preview: Long and Steady Workouts

Workout	Distance (miles)	Total workout time (min)	Walking time (min)	Intensity (% max HR/RPE)
1	3	60	45	75-79/5
2	3½	65	49	75-79/5
3	4	70-75	56-57	75-79/5
4	4½	75-80	60-67	75-79/5
5	5	85	70	80-84/6
6	6	85-110	84-90	80-89/6
7	6.2	95-105	80-87	75-94/5-8
8	7	95-120	91-105	80-84/6
9	9.3	120-155	120-139	75-94/5-8
10	10	140-155	130-140	80-84/6
11	11	140-155	140-150	80-84/6
12	13.1	175-195	157-183	80-94/6-8

Workout 1

Total time: 60 minutes

Warm-up: Walk for 5 to 7 minutes at a pace slower than your goal pace, relaxing your shoulders and visualizing your success at this first longer walk. Stretch if desired.

Workout

Distance	3 miles
Walking time	45 minutes
Pace	15-minute miles
Heart zone	75 to 79% max HR
Effort	RPE 5

Cool-down: Walk easily for 5 to 7 minutes, then stretch.

Calories used: 270

Comments: Don't push yourself to go too fast, especially in the beginning when you feel fresh. The goal is to finish feeling energized. If you're using many of the workouts in chapter 7 (medium and steady) for your baseline, you may want to slow this workout to 16- or 17-minute miles, but keep it well paced.

Workout 2

Total time: 65 minutes

Warm-up: Walk for 5 to 7 minutes at a pace slower than your goal pace, relaxing your shoulders. Stretch if desired.

Workout

Distance	3½ miles
Walking time	49 minutes
Pace	15-minute miles
Heart zone	75 to 79% max HR
Effort	RPE 5

Cool-down: Walk easily for 5 to 7 minutes, then stretch.

Calories used: 295

Comments: Don't increase the distance or speed of your long walk until you're comfortable with workout 1. With this one, try to start with a faster pace, then let yourself slow in the last half so that you average about 15-minute miles. Use the same rule of thumb if your average pace is going to be a bit faster or slower. Remember, the push-off from the toe of the back foot remains strong now, even on flat terrain.

Workout 3

Total time: 70 to 75 minutes

Warm-up: Walk for 5 to 7 minutes at a pace slower than your goal pace, sensing the rolling motion in your feet. Stretch if desired.

Workout

Distance	4 miles
Walking time	56 to 57 minutes
Pace	14- to 15-minute miles
Heart zone	75 to 79% max HR
Effort	RPE 5

Cool-down: Walk easily for 5 to 7 minutes, then stretch.

Calories used: 360

Comments: Tackle this workout with the intention of completing the entire distance at a steady clip. Now that these workouts at a steady pace are heading toward an hour, you might want to find a friend to walk with.

Workout 4

Total time: 75 to 80 minutes

Warm-up: Walk for 5 to 7 minutes at a pace slower than your goal pace, sensing the rolling motion in your feet from heel to toe. Stretch if desired.

Workout

Distance	4½ miles
Walking time	60 to 67 minutes
Pace	14- to 15-minute miles
Heart zone	75 to 79% max HR
Effort	RPE 5

Cool-down: Walk easily for 5 to 7 minutes, then stretch.

Calories used: 415

Comments: If you can complete this workout walking 14-minute miles, then you'll be done in an hour. A pretty nice accomplishment for only an hour of your time!

Workout 5

Total time: 85 minutes

Warm-up: Walk for 5 to 7 minutes at an easy pace, stretch, then walk another 2 to 3 minutes at a more moderate pace.

Workout

Distance	5 miles
Walking time	70 minutes
Pace	14-minute miles
Heart zone	80 to 84% max HR
Effort	RPE 6

Cool-down: Walk easily for ½ mile, then stretch.

Calories used: 465

Comments: If you are a more advanced athletic walker whose daily workouts cover about 5 miles, then you can use this as a general workout several times a week when you can't or don't feel like doing anything speedier but want to keep the pace going. Be sure to cover the entire distance, slowing to a perceived exertion of 4 to 5 if you need to.

Workout 6

Total time: 85 to 110 minutes

Warm-up: Walk for 5 to 7 minutes at an easy pace, stretch, then walk another 2 to 3 minutes at a more moderate pace. See comments.

Workout

Distance	6 miles
Walking time	84 to 90 minutes
Pace	14- to 15-minute miles
Heart zone	80 to 89% max HR
Effort	RPE 6

Cool-down: Walk easily for ½ mile, then stretch. See comments.

Calories used: 565

Comments: With this workout you can start at a slower and easier pace, stopping to stretch after about 5 minutes, then launch back into the rest of your walk. You don't need an entirely separate warm-up, which will shorten your total time, too. The same applies to the cool-down: Just slow to an easier pace for the last few minutes. This workout gives you a chance to push to the 14s as a test of what you can do.

Workout 7

Total time: 95 to 105 minutes

Warm-up: Walk for about a mile at an easy pace, stretch, then walk another 3 to 4 minutes at a faster pace.

Workout

Distance	6.2 miles (10 kilometers)
Walking time	80 to 87 minutes
Pace	13- to 14-minute miles
Heart zone	75 to 94% max HR
Effort	RPE 5 to 8 (see page 125 in the introduction for an explanation of the wide range of effort)

Cool-down: Walk easily for ½ mile, then stretch.

Calories used: 620

Comments: Find a local 10-kilometer run for this workout. The energy of the pack will keep you going. Pick an event with markers every mile and someone calling out times. That'll help you keep your pace. Don't start out too fast. And don't worry about being last; joggers can run pretty slowly! Remember, either use the spirit of the event to push you harder than usual, or walk your normal pace and enjoy the company and water stations.

Workout 8

Total time: 95 to 120 minutes

Warm-up: Walk for 7 to 10 minutes at an easy pace, stretch, then walk another 3 to 4 minutes at a more moderate pace.

Workout

Distance	7 miles
Walking time	91 to 105 minutes
Pace	13- to 15-minute miles
Heart zone	80 to 84% max HR
Effort	RPE 6

Cool-down: Walk easily for ½ mile, then stretch.

Calories used: 665

Comments: You should be able to accomplish workout 6 before adding the extra mile to get to this distance. If you need to ease off the pace to a perceived exertion of 4 or 5 to be able to complete the distance, by all means do it. And as with all other long workouts, you can warm up during the first part of the workout, if desired, which will shorten the total workout time. Be sure to take the day off or do only a very easy workout the day after this long walk.

Workout 9

Total time: 120 to 155 minutes

Warm-up: Walk for about a mile at an easy pace, stretch, then walk another 3 to 4 minutes at a faster pace, or incorporate the warm-up into the first part of the workout by starting slowly.

Workout

Distance	9.3 miles (15 kilometers)
Walking time	120 to 139 minutes
Pace	13- to 15-minute miles
Heart zone	75 to 94% max HR
Effort	RPE 5 to 8 (see page 125 in the introduction for an explanation of the wide range of effort)

Cool-down: Walk easily for ½ mile, then stretch.

Calories used: 940

Comments: Look for a 15-kilometer race (9.3 miles), which will be harder to find than the omnipresent 10-kilometer events. If need be, substitute a 12-kilometer (7.4-mile) running race or find your own route on a marked trail and note your time. You can also complete a 10-kilometer race, and then keep walking for another 3 miles after the finish. Admittedly, that can be hard to do, but it's worth a try. Forget about demanding workouts for a week after this workout to give your body a chance to recover. Use the race to urge your body to go faster than normal or as a great way to do a long walk with a bunch of people.

Workout 10

Total time: 140 to 155 minutes

Warm-up: Walk for 7 to 10 minutes at an easy pace, stretch, then walk another 3 to 4 minutes at a more moderate pace, or simply start your walk more slowly, gradually picking up the pace.

Workout

Distance	10 miles
Walking time	130 to 140 minutes
Pace	13- to 14-minute miles
Heart zone	80 to 84% max HR
Effort	RPE 6

Cool-down: Walk easily for ½ mile, then stretch.

Calories used: 1,010

Comments: Doing longer workouts can make you faster at shorter distances. For example, this workout is great if you want to feel like you can breeze through a 10-kilometer race comfortably. Keep the pace steady, but if you need to, go ahead and slow your pace and perceived exertion slightly so you can finish the entire distance.

Workout 11

Total time: 140 to 155 minutes

Warm-up: Once your workouts reach this length, use the first few minutes as your warm-up, stop to stretch, then continue at your intended pace.

Workout

Distance	11 miles
Walking time	140 to 150 minutes
Pace	13- to 14-minute miles
Heart zone	80 to 84% max HR
Effort	RPE 6

Cool-down: Walk easily for ½ mile or a bit farther, then stretch.

Calories used: 1,100 (up to 250 more with hills)

Comments: Like workout 11, this will give you more strength to complete shorter distances at faster paces much more comfortably. A 3-mile walk won't feel like much of a workout after you can do this kind of distance! Don't forget to refuel and rehydrate. For more variety, try tackling this workout over rolling hills, really pushing up the incline and relaxing down the other side. If you need to, slow your pace over the hills to keep your perceived effort from skyrocketing.

Workout 12

Total time: 175 to 195 minutes

Warm-up: Walk for about a mile at an easy pace, stretch, then walk another 3 to 4 minutes at a faster pace, or incorporate the warm-up into the first part of the race by starting slowly and gradually speeding up. However, if you intend to race this, you need to be fully warmed up and eagerly toeing the starting line.

Workout

Distance	13.1 miles (half-marathon)
Walking time	157 to 183 minutes
Pace	12- to 14-minute miles
Heart zone	80 to 94% max HR
Effort	RPE 6 to 8

Cool-down: Walk easily for ½ mile to a mile, then stretch.

Calories used: 1,325

Comments: The urge will be, as at all starting lines, to start too fast. Avoid this temptation by burying yourself in the middle or back of the pack. You *won't* be able to go too fast until the racers thin out. Remember to drink the water and carbohydrate beverages provided along the route (or take your own) because your muscles will start craving energy after about 90 minutes. It's at this time that you're at risk of hitting the wall, so don't wait until your energy has crashed before trying to reload. It takes a while for your body to assimilate it. And don't get so caught up in finish festivities that you forget to stretch. If you can't find a half-marathon, try a 20-kilometer race (12.4 miles). You may also want to find a friend to accompany you. You'll feel empowered after you complete this distance!

III

The Programs

Parts I and II covered fitness checkups, walking technique, gearing up, how to train safely, and 60 workouts of various levels and types. Now you're prepared to start a new walking program or reinvigorate a stale routine. The following chapters explain how to structure a workout program based on your fitness level, needs, and other cross-training desires or environmental limitations.

Why Follow a Walking Program?

A structured program is not just for an athlete with Olympic aspirations but can help anybody set off on the right foot and keep going. Sure, you can work out with no particular concept of time or mileage a few times a week and still improve your fitness and health. But adding structure to your workouts will take you farther a lot faster and keep you interested and motivated. Think of your workout program as your own personal walking trainer. Everyone needs guidance now and then, and that's what the programs in this book provide. The variety in a structured program is more interesting than simply stepping out the door and striding along for a half hour every now and then.

Combining appropriate workouts at the appropriate level with self-discipline and patience will help you maintain or improve your health and fitness and explore your walking potential. Notice I say *potential,* not goal. That's because one goal can be too limiting and too specific. Your potential, on the other hand, can be bottomless, and it is based entirely on your abilities and your needs, which can change from day to day, from year to year, from mood to mood. Certainly setting short-term goals can help you along. But they must be addressed constantly and not become stagnant. If you sit back and say you've reached your goal and you're now done reaching, you've given up on yourself and your potential. Keep reaching, I say. That's what these programs are all about: helping you continue to reach and explore the options and adventures that await you on every walk.

Three Levels of Programs

The walking programs are organized into three levels, each with specific characteristics based on three broad goals that tend to encompass most exercisers. Choose the workout programs that fit your style or desires, which of course may change at any time or as you progress!

1. **Health Walking.** This category fits many people. You may be new to exercise and want to lose weight or lower your blood cholesterol levels. You may have been injured and need to ease slowly back into exercise. Perhaps you used to exercise but haven't for years and would like to start again. You probably don't expect to walk more than 1 to 3 miles, two or three times a week, with an occasional easy weekend workout up to 4 miles. Many of your workouts will be at a strolling pace. Time and pace won't be as much of a concern to you, although this program provides a few guidelines.

2. **Fitness Walking.** If you walk three or four times a week, perhaps covering 3 to 5 miles each time, usually choose slightly brisker walks, think about your time and pace a bit, and maybe dabble in an athletic walk or even a few longer weekend outings, this level is right for you. You may satisfy your fitness needs with this program alone. But you might also be an exerciser who uses walking to fill gaps between other activities—working out at a health club, taking aerobics or martial arts classes, riding a bicycle, even running. Either way, walking is an important part of your regimen or might be your entire fitness program.

3. **Athletic Walking.** You are a serious walker. This is your sport and you are very dedicated. You proudly identify walking as what you do. Your walking workouts average 4 to 6 miles, five or six days a week, with some longer jaunts here and there, maybe even *much* longer on the weekend. Perhaps you already compete in walking, you've thought about it, or you simply feel a bit competitive when you take part in a weekend walk event. You've taken part in or considered a half-marathon or even a marathon. And you probably keep one eye on your watch as you walk. Most of your workouts are athletic walks with even hints of race walking.

Selecting Your Program

Although the workout chapters are arranged by type, with the workouts in each chapter listed in ascending order of difficulty or length or both, the workouts are meant to be mixed and matched. Select workouts from several chapters to accommodate your needs or time constraints.

Truly novice health walkers may stick mostly to workouts in the short and easy chapter, and then try a few from the medium and steady and long and steady workouts as their walking program and fitness level progress. Fitness, or intermediate walkers might find the most satisfaction from medium and steady or medium and quicker workouts, with occasional forays into long and steady or, for a new challenge, short and fast, as well as a few short and easy workouts for a quick noontime break. The program for an athletic, or advanced, walker might include workouts from a wide range of categories, with medium and steady, medium and quicker, and long and steady workouts making up the bulk of the program, plus a few short and fast workouts or even a short and easy walk the day after an intense effort.

If you are still unsure of which program fits you, use these suggestions to help you decide:

- Review the material and fitness checkups in chapter 1 now that you've read the subsequent materials and glanced at the workouts themselves.
- Take another look at the descriptions for health, fitness, or athletic walking in the introduction to part I, and select where you think you belong.
- Go back for a peek at the introduction to part II and review the descriptions of each type of workout, then thumb through the workouts to see which workouts may tantalize you or suit you the best.

Another factor in choosing a base program is to know yourself. You need to recognize what you want to achieve through your program: simply strolling a couple of easy miles three times a week, briskly striding 14- or 15-minute miles for 45 minutes four times a week, or being able to breeze through a truly athletic 11- or 12-minute mile without huffing and panting, and passing joggers in weekend races.

No matter where you start or where you decide you belong, the combinations are infinite. Fully explore them and fully enjoy them. Remember, the examples are only a springboard, intended to introduce you to the concept of using this book as a workout smorgasbord. You can change levels at any time. You may choose health walking, then find that you're really beyond that. No problem, try a few fitness walking workouts. Or, maybe you eagerly jumped straight into athletic walking, but those workouts were too much. Again, no problem, slide yourself back into the fitness walking workouts.

Chapter 11 contains two 4-week programs for each of the three levels as samples for combining the workouts into a program. You can create your own programs or simply repeat these month after month. Chapter 12 contains cross-training walking programs based on the programs in chapter 11. These suggest where, when, and what you could do on certain days besides simply walking. Also included is advice on how to determine your effort level, pace, or workout times during these other activities. Chapter 12 also includes several new cross-training programs that you can now better understand after seeing how the original walking programs were modified. In Chapter 13, it all comes together as you learn how to design your own program. You also learn how to modify a program when other responsibilities get in the way. Because life happens: business travel, vacations, family outings, summer vacation with the kids at home, rainy winters, hot summers, snowy streets, and the like. There's no reason to hang it up at those times. Just get creative and modify, modify, modify.

CHAPTER 11

Walking Programs

Here you will find six 4-week sample programs, two each for health walkers (novice or easy level), fitness walkers (frequent or moderate level), and athletic walkers (advanced or intense level). The two programs within each category are graduated. For example, health walking program I is slightly easier than health walking program II. Each sample shows workout days and rest days. Listed with each workout day are symbols that correspond to the names of the workouts described in part II:

Workout Program Key

short and easy (SE)   short and fast (SF)

medium and steady (MS)   long and steady (LS)

medium and quicker (MQ)

The number after the letters refers to the specific numbered workout within each level.

Using the Programs Wisely

Although rest days are delineated, you can of course shift the workout days one way or the other. For example, I've slated Sunday as the off-day in all programs because I've found over the years that family obligations can make Sundays less convenient for workouts or simply because it's nice to end your weekend with a day off. But, that's not set in stone! If you *like* to get in a workout before the workweek strikes, by all means shift the workouts over a day so that Monday becomes your regular day off. The only caveat is that rest days have been worked into the programs with care so that they occur before or after more difficult workouts. Therefore, don't substitute a rest day with a workout or shift two workouts together, eliminating the rest day.

I've also graduated the miles walked and the type of workouts in each program. Each workout has a certain speed associated with it, but if your body would rather go a bit faster or a bit slower, go for it. The workouts are designed to adapt to your needs. The four-week program has also been designed in a progression from week to week, graduating miles and level. Therefore, if one week is too challenging as you move along, stick with that week of the program for another week, or more, until it becomes more comfortable, then move on to the next week. When you finish the first four weeks and you feel comfortably challenged—it wasn't too easy or too overwhelming—you can move into the second four weeks for that level. If you're not satisfied with how it feels but aren't ready to move up a level, simply repeat the same four-week program before you move along.

Once you can easily handle the second program in a level, move straight into the first program of the next level. In other words, these six programs could be considered one long series of six, 4-week programs, with each week or each month repeatable as desired, if the goal of each level fits your needs and lifestyle.

In the programs that follow, the weekly mileage does not include the warm-up and cool-down distances since these amounts may vary depending on your goals, level, and time constraints.

Health Walking Programs

Many health walkers will be able to start with medium and steady workouts, then be able to tackle medium and quicker workouts in no time. The short and easy workouts are very comfortable and will suit you best if you're completely new to movement, haven't enjoyed regular activity in many years, or have taken time off because of an injury. Despite their ease, the short and easy workouts are great simple workouts not to be neglected.

Health walkers in the beginning program walk two or three times a week, eventually shooting for three, and take at least one day off between workouts. They cover 2 to 10 miles a week.

PROGRAM I

The first sample program is for the newly active person. It is designed to ease you into walking, mixing small amounts of short and easy walking with lots of rest.

Health Walking I

	Sun	Mon	Tues	Wed	Thurs	Fri	Sat	Total miles
Week 1	Rest	SE4	Rest	SE5	Rest	Rest	SE7	4.0
Week 2	Rest	SE6	Rest	SE9	Rest	SE7	Rest	4¾
Week 3	Rest	SE9	Rest	Rest	SE11	Rest	MS1	5.0
Week 4	Rest	Rest	SE12	Rest	MS1	Rest	MS2	5¾

PROGRAM II

This program is slightly more strenuous than the first, adding longer and slightly more intense workouts. Although it's also geared toward beginners, it's not appropriate for someone who is unprepared or has never exercised. This program requires that you have several weeks of walking under your belt and be able to easily pace off a mile before attempting it.

Health Walking II

	Sun	Mon	Tues	Wed	Thurs	Fri	Sat	Total miles
Week 1	Rest	Rest	SE11	Rest	SE12	Rest	MS6	6¼
Week 2	Rest	SE7	Rest	SE12	Rest	Rest	LS1	6¾
Week 3	Rest	Rest	MS2	Rest	MS3	Rest	MS7	7.0
Week 4	Rest	MS6	Rest	Rest	MS4	Rest	LS1	7¾

Fitness Walking Programs

Medium and steady and medium and quicker workouts, with a long and steady workout on the weekend, will meet the needs of most fitness walkers. Still, they might want to try an occasional short and fast walk, or slip in an easy jaunt on a rest day.

This program includes three or four workouts a week. Rest days are still important, but you might walk two days in a row, with the second day much easier than the first. You will cover 10 to 20 miles a week, and the more advanced fitness walkers will be able to complete weekend fun walks of about 3 miles (5 kilometers).

Because fitness walking and athletic walking are more intense than health walking, the last week of each of the four-week cycles is a down week. This week totals about 20 to 30 percent less mileage and usually includes an extra day off. This should refresh you mentally and physically before you start a new four-week cycle.

PROGRAM I

This first sample program meets all-around exercise needs.

Fitness Walking I

	Sun	Mon	Tues	Wed	Thurs	Fri	Sat	Total miles
Week 1	Rest	MS7	Rest	MS8	MS1	Rest	LS3	12.0
Week 2	Rest	Rest	MQ5	Rest	MQ11	MQ1	LS4	13.0
Week 3	Rest	MQ5	Rest	MQ4	Rest	MS11	LS5	14½
Week 4	Rest	Rest	MQ4	Rest	MS9	Rest	MQ9	9.1*

*This is the down week, which ends with a 5-kilometer event. This easier week should allow you to start the race more rested. Your mileage this week may actually be a mile or so higher if you include a warm-up and cool-down for the event.

PROGRAM II

This second program builds additional strength with a touch of speed. Advanced walkers can also use one or two weeks of this program when they feel the need for simpler workouts.

Fitness Walking II

	Sun	Mon	Tues	Wed	Thurs	Fri	Sat	Total miles
Week 1	Rest	MS10	Rest	SF3	MQ5	Rest	LS5	13¾
Week 2	Rest	MS11	Rest	MQ4	MQ5	Rest	LS7	15.20*
Week 3	Rest	MQ8	SF5	Rest	MS12	Rest	LS6	15¼
Week 4	Rest	MS10	Rest	MS11	Rest	Rest	MQ10	10.85**

*This week ends with a 6.2-mile (10-kilometer) weekend event, which you can do as a slightly up-tempo longer workout. You may end up warming up, which will increase the weekly mileage a bit. Or, you can start more slowly and pick up the pace after 5 to 10 minutes.

**This is the down week, which also ends in a 5-kilometer weekend event. Total mileage will likely be higher, depending on how much warm-up and cool-down you do for the event.

Athletic Walking Programs

Advanced walkers, even if they never compete formally, often keep one eye on their watch and compete with themselves. Athletic walkers choose mostly medium and quicker and short and fast workouts, with a good dash of long and steady. Medium and steady workouts add variety and provide an easier workout after a more intense challenge. The right combination of workouts will help advanced walkers improve personal performances and be ready for many weekend 10K walks.

Advanced walkers work out five or six days a week, and they have the strength to walk on back-to-back days. But both back-to-back workouts should not be intense. Advanced walkers cover 20 to 35 miles a week.

PROGRAM I

This first program mixes most types of workouts. Although some weeks have three or five days back-to-back, they are arranged to include easier days in the series. Avoid changing the order, otherwise you might overdo it.

Athletic Walking I

	Sun	Mon	Tues	Wed	Thurs	Fri	Sat	Total miles
Week 1	Rest	MQ12	LS3	Rest	SF5	MS9	LS6	20.0
Week 2	Rest	MQ5	SF8	SE12	MS11	MQ11	LS8	22½
Week 3	Rest	MS10	MQ5	LS5	Rest	MS9	LS9	24½*
Week 4	Rest	Rest	LS5	SF6	Rest	MS12	LS6	18¼**

*This week ends with a 15-kilometer (9.3-mile) distance event. These can be difficult to find, but because it's just a long workout, you can always do it on your own and round the distance up or down slightly, or you could do a 10-kilometer (6.2-mile) event and add another loop.

**This is the down week of the cycle. Note that it includes just four workouts and the long workout is shorter than usual to help you recover.

PROGRAM II

This second advanced walking program builds on the first to increase mileage and allow you to work toward walking a half-marathon. If you don't want to complete a half-marathon, substitute that event with a long workout. But keep in mind that it is nice to have a goal. If you do plan to aim for a half-marathon, diligently follow the full eight weeks of the athletic program. In fact, it's a good idea to repeat another four weeks to finish three months of solid training before the event. If your goal in the event is just to make a long walk of it, eight weeks should be fine. If you want to *race* it, walking harder than normal, schedule a practice event, then keep training another month or so before the real thing.

Athletic Walking II

	Sun	Mon	Tues	Wed	Thurs	Fri	Sat	Total miles
Week 1	Rest	LS5	MQ5	LS5	Rest	LS5	LS8	25.0
Week 2	Rest	MQ11	LS6	SF9	MS12	Rest	LS10	26¾
Week 3	Rest	SF9	LS6	MS9	LS5	MS12	LS8	28¼
Week 4	Rest	MS11	SF5	Rest	SE12	Rest	LS12	21.6*

*This week concludes with the half-marathon. Your weekly mileage may end up being a mile or so higher, depending on how much warm-up and cool-down you do.

Marathon Training

A lot of walkers are diving into marathon training programs and marathons themselves. This book is not intended or designed to lay out programs to get you to that 26.2-mile distance. That is not to say that you couldn't use the information and techniques in these pages to support your program. This book can be useful, and the base workouts can provide a good start to your training. It's just that you need to continue the mileage progression until your longest once-a-week workout is about 20 miles, with weekly mileage anywhere from 40 to 60 miles.

Before you embark on the adventure of a marathon and training for it, you must be able to walk briskly three or four times a week, covering about 15 miles. And you should do that for at least six months. Preparing for a marathon takes at least four months and optimally six. Marathon programs exist that promise to get you safely to the starting line in three or four months, starting from scratch. I don't agree with that philosophy and believe that those programs run the risk of setting you up for injury, burnout, and a less-than-successful marathon experience. Do it smartly, do it well, and do it safely, and you'll remember the experience positively for a long time.

Now that you've pondered pure walking programs, the next chapter shows you how to modify them slightly to add cross-training days for variety.

Cross-Training Walking Programs

Walking is a superior activity for improving fitness and health. But sometimes you need or want to mix it up a little by adding other activities to your foundation of walking workouts. Or sometimes another activity simply sounds like fun every now and then. Cross-training, and the motivation it provides, can be the answer.

In chapter 5, I discussed supplements to a walking program, including the warm-up, cool-down, and strengthening components. I also introduced a basic but adventure-inspiring menu of cross-training activities, from those that are walking-based (for example, Nordic walking) to those that are not (such as group exercise or cycling). Although you are a walker, or are becoming one, being familiar with how to add cross-training to your walking program will be a benefit when you need or want to take a break from walking. The following series of walking program examples show you how to add one or two workouts a week from the cross-training menu.

You don't have to use these programs as stand-alone four-week packages that must be done in their entirety. Rather, think of these as an example of the choices available and as a way to learn how to modify your walking program. For example, you could choose to take one or two weeks of an appropriate program and complete it as it is presented. Or you could take the concepts and apply them to your own needs. The sky's the limit when it comes to making choices that will make your program work for you and easy to maintain.

How to Choose Activities

Start thinking about what you might choose from chapter 5 and how to include it. What you select as a cross-training activity depends not only on your personal tastes but also on your ability, experience, geographic location, time constraints, available equipment and clubs, and perhaps the desires of friends and family who might want you as company.

I am frequently asked how long to do X activity to equal the benefit gained and calories used in Y activity. Of course, you can use all kinds of complicated metabolic equations, and you can split hairs about whether you need to do a few minutes more or less. But, really, how to approach an activity comes down to three factors, pure and simple. These were discussed in-depth in chapter 4:

1. Your heart rate
2. Your perceived effort
3. Time spent in the activity

Why these three things? Because if you *feel* about the same in X activity as you normally do in Y activity, you give both activities the same effort rating. And if your heart rate during the activities is comparable, you are likely getting a similar training effect and, therefore, similar improvements in fitness and similar calorie use. Note the word *similar.* These activities aren't the same, just close enough for most people. If you really want to know exact differences in calorie use and physiology, there are plenty of books—much more technical than this one—that break it down for you. Otherwise, just realize that if the effort is approximately the same, the benefits are about the same.

But what if you do something that feels more difficult or less difficult? Use your head. If it's more difficult, you won't need to do it for as long to reach a similar training effect. For example, if you run one day a week and your perceived exertion is 7 instead of 5, then you might feel you've gotten your fill after 30 minutes compared to the 45 minutes you'd normally walk.

On the other hand, if the activity feels easier, then you can go longer and farther to achieve the results you might desire. In this case, if you are used to walking vigorously for an hour, but instead go for a long and more leisurely bike ride, you may want to ride for 90 minutes or even two hours (depending on how leisurely that leisurely pace is).

The goal is to enjoy the activity you undertake so that you want to do it and don't end up thinking about it like some kind of medical prescription or drudgery that makes you watch the second hand on your watch.

Bicycling is a great cross-training activity that provides a break from your usual routine and works a different set of muscles.

Table 12.1 lists sample aerobic activities listed in chapter 5, each labeled and numbered with a code. A stands for aerobic, and W stands for walking. You'll find these codes, for example, A3 or W4, mixed in with the walking workouts in the sample programs that start on page 157.

Sample Cross-Training Programs

In chapter 11, I laid out two sample four-week programs for each of the three levels—health walking, fitness walking, and athletic walking. In this chapter, I have provided two more programs for each level that incorporate cross-training activities geared toward walkers of that level with their typical goals and strengths in mind. The first program in each level takes one of the programs from chapter 11 and includes notations about where you might replace a walking workout with cross-training activities. These are labeled program I and illustrate how cross-training fits into a regular walking program you already know.

Program II lets you take the cross-training concept to the next level on your own. These ready-to-use programs provide an additional example of how to intersperse nonwalking activities into your workout for a more varied program.

Table 12.1 Aerobically oriented activities

Walking activities	Aerobic activities
W1 Nordic walking	A1 Outdoor bicycling
W2 Retro walking	A2 Group exercise
W3 Run-walking	A3 Indoor equipment
W4 Snowshoeing	A4 Swimming
W5 Outdoor circuit training	A5 Hiking
	A6 Water running or walking
	A7 Yoga, Pilates, or tai chi
	A8 Cross-country skiing
	A9 Running or jogging

Health Walking Cross-Training Programs

Because a health walker is a walking beginner and activity novice, or might need or want an easier or lower-impact exercise, activities like running won't be considered. Instead, possible options will be low- or nonimpact and easily accomplished without a lot of gear.

PROGRAM I

This first program builds on the second tier of the novice programs for health walkers. Because a health walker works out only three times a week in this program, I've included only one day of cross-training. The fourth week includes two days for an additional break for the body.

Health Walking Cross-Training Program I

	Sun	Mon	Tues	Wed	Thurs	Fri	Sat
Week 1	Rest	Rest	SE11	Rest	SE12	Rest	MS6 / A1
Week 2	Rest	SE7	Rest	SE12 / A2	Rest	Rest	LS1
Week 3	Rest	Rest	SE12	Rest	MS2 / A7	Rest	MS7
Week 4	Rest	MS6 / A6	Rest	Rest	MS4 / A5	Rest	LS1

PROGRAM II

The second cross-training program in the health walking category follows the same formula as in the first cross-training program. Whereas the first one simply modifies a program you know from chapter 11, this one adds low-impact, nonwalking activities to an all-new program still geared for novices or those doing mostly easier workouts. This program also includes one cross-training workout in the first three weeks and two in the last week.

Health Walking Cross-Training Program II

	Sun	Mon	Tues	Wed	Thurs	Fri	Sat
Week 1	Rest	SE6	Rest	A4	Rest	SE7	Rest
Week 2	Rest	Rest	SE10	Rest	A3	Rest	MS4
Week 3	Rest	Rest	A7	Rest	SE12	Rest	MS3
Week 4	Rest	A1	Rest	Rest	SE9	Rest	A2

Fitness Walking Cross-Training Programs

A fitness walker can participate in a lot of different activities at a brisk level, a level that is not too hard, but not too easy. With only equipment, weather, and geographic location as deciding factors, a fitness walker can choose just about any activity. And with basic fitness as a goal, mixing up activities that use different muscles in different ways offers many benefits.

PROGRAM I

This program builds on the second tier of the fitness walking programs from chapter 11 by adding cross-training options. Because fitness walkers work out four days a week, two days each week are possible cross-training days, while in the fourth "down" week, only one day is for cross-training because the walking workouts have already been minimized. In the third week I pretended that you were on a long winter weekend in the mountains, and I scheduled two winter activities. You can substitute them with the others noted in parentheses.

Fitness Walking Cross-Training Program I

	Sun	Mon	Tues	Wed	Thurs	Fri	Sat
Week 1	Rest	MS10 / W1	Rest	SF3	MQ5 / A2	Rest	LS5
Week 2	Rest	MS11 / A5	Rest	MQ4 / A7	MQ5	Rest	LS7
Week 3	Rest	MQ8	SF5	Rest	MS12 / A8 (A5)	Rest	LS6 / W4 (A1)
Week 4	Rest	MS10	Rest	MS11 / A3	Rest	Rest	MQ10

PROGRAM II

This second program follows the same principles that guide the first. Look for alternate activities appearing twice a week during the first three weeks and only once during the fourth week. Because you are a moderate and regular exerciser, the sky is the limit on what you choose.

Fitness Walking Cross-Training Program II

	Sun	Mon	Tues	Wed	Thurs	Fri	Sat
Week 1	Rest	W5	Rest	MS7	A6	Rest	LS6
Week 2	Rest	MS8	Rest	A4	MQ4	Rest	A5
Week 3	Rest	LS1	Rest	A9	Rest	MS12	A7
Week 4	Rest	Rest	A2	Rest	LS3	Rest	LS5

Athletic Walking Cross-Training Programs

An athletic walker is in much more advanced shape physically and can therefore tackle many different activities, even at much higher levels of exertion. Aside from weather, location, and geography, which workout to choose may come down to personal taste. I have assumed that the athletic walker enjoys the walking motion, so therefore have suggested alternatives that are similar.

PROGRAM I

This cross-training program is adapted from the athletic walker's program I in chapter 11. With five or six walking workouts in a week, two cross-training days provide a good alternative. But, as with the fitness walkers, only one cross-training workout is scheduled in the fourth week because it already contains fewer walking workouts.

Athletic Walking Cross-Training Program I

	Sun	Mon	Tues	Wed	Thurs	Fri	Sat
Week 1	Rest	MQ12	LS3 / A9	Rest	SF5 / A2	MS9	LS6
Week 2	Rest	MQ5	SF8	SE12 / A1	MS11 / W1 (W4)	MQ11	LS8
Week 3	Rest	MS10 / A9	MQ5	LS5 / A5	Rest	MS9	LS9
Week 4	Rest	Rest	LS5 / W3	SF6	Rest	MS12	LS6

PROGRAM II

Because athletic walkers are passionate exercisers, they have a larger range of cross-training alternatives. Experiment as much as you want; just make sure you schedule enough rest and don't do strenuous walking workouts and strenuous alternative workouts back to back. Variety is what you'll see in this second program.

Athletic Walking Cross-Training Program II

	Sun	Mon	Tues	Wed	Thurs	Fri	Sat
Week 1	Rest	MQ11	W3 / W2	Rest	MS11	A3	SE12
Week 2	Rest	LS3	Rest	A6	MQ5	A7	SF6
Week 3	Rest	MS9	W1	Rest	LS4	MQ8	A1
Week 4	Rest	A9	Rest	SF5	LS2	Rest	MQ9

As you can see, the possibilities are endless. There are so many ways to spice up your walking program that you should feel like a kid in a candy shop. What to choose? Where to go next? It all looks so good! Recognizing your activity options can be invaluable when other demands make if difficult to go out for your usual walking workout. A broader view of what your exercise program entails will make it easier for you to keep at it, in some way, even if a walk isn't on the horizon. That broader view will help keep you active for life. And keeping active for life is what it's all about.

13

Program Customization

We're coming into the homestretch, and now it's time to let go of your personal trainer's hand and take a few steps on your own. Here is where I will teach you guidelines for how to set up your own program and how to work through the hurdles in your normal routine, such as vacations and business travel, that can throw off your best-laid workout plans. Knowing a few tricks can keep you active despite interruptions, especially if you understand the fundamentals of your program and its development.

General Guidelines

The guidelines for each type of walker—health, fitness, and athletic—are slightly different and based on each group's fitness level and ability. Although these are clearly specified, it's important to remember that rules are made to be broken. If you fall between two groups, need to ease up, or want to put the pedal down, it's up to you to understand your body, your needs, and your preferences, and then implement a plan that will allow you to meet your walking potential.

This chapter on program development is not intended to be a technically detailed explanation of cycles, phases, and mileage buildup for complicated routines for advanced walkers. For that, my *Walking Fast* book (Human Kinetics, 1998) fills the bill. This chapter provides a basic approach for anyone who wants to wisely choose his or her own workouts for a program that progresses toward the goal of getting and staying active, fit, and healthy.

Basic and more complicated programs both follow nearly the same guidelines. After you read through the list that follows, and as you prepare to plot your own program, you can refer to the sample programs in chapter 11 to see how these guidelines shaped the structure. Although you probably didn't see the pattern when you first read through them, you'll recognize their influence now.

- **Build mileage by 10 to 20 percent a week.** Increasing your mileage by more than that could lead to injury or burnout. Novice walkers should stick closer to 10 percent, while those with more experience may slide toward 15 to 20 percent a week.

- **Think in blocks of four weeks.** Everyone, except a novice health walker, should build their mileage slightly over a three-week period, then drop it by 10 to 20 percent in the fourth week before moving ahead again. The "down" week provides a great physical and mental break. Because health walkers only work out three times a week, they can simply lower their mileage a bit, but only if they feel the need for a break.

- **Add race events only about once a month.** Weekend fun runs can be inspiring and a lot of fun, not to mention social, too. But they can be stressful if you get caught up in all the people and excitement and walk more intensely or more briskly than you should. But if you can keep your excitement in check and walk your own pace, then including one in your program once every month or two gives you something to look forward to. If you have the temperament to cruise along without competing, then you can enter more. Know thyself and schedule wisely.

- **Think hard–easy.** A walker at any level (or runner or athlete of any kind) lives by the hard–easy rule. If you do a harder or longer workout one day, the next day should either be off (a novice walker on a three-day weekly program) or easier or shorter (fitness and athletic walkers). This allows your body, and muscles, and other systems to recover properly.

- **Temper your enthusiasm.** Doing too much, too soon, too frequently only leads to injury, dropout, and burnout. This is particularly true for novice exercisers. That's partly because the soft tissue (muscles, ligaments, and tendons) isn't accustomed to an activity, so while the heart and lungs are telling you, "Hey, this is easy, let's do more," your soft tissue is quietly suffering. The problem is, it will often only start talking once the damage has been done, which is usually after about four to eight weeks. So do your long-term goals a huge favor and temper your enthusiasm. Time is your friend.

Level-Specific Guidelines

Now that the general guidelines are laid out, it's time to take a look at specific guidelines for each level. These include a summary of each level plus the workout guidelines for each level in a nutshell. These will be simple to refer to as you fill in the blanks in your program.

Health Walking

If you are a health walker, you are new to walking and most likely somewhat new to exercise too. Your emphasis is on improving health (such as blood cholesterol or weight loss) and not on performance.

Frequency: Two or three times a week

Mileage per workout: 1 to 3 miles

Long walk: 3 to 4 miles

Weekly mileage: 2 to 10 miles

For example, your walking days in the first week on your customized program might look like this:

	Sun	Mon	Tues	Wed	Thurs	Fri	Sat	Total miles
Week 1	Rest	Walk	Rest	Rest	Walk	Rest	Walk	4

Fitness Walking

You are a fitness walker if you are moderately and regularly active. You may still work on your health or weight, but you're also interested in improving your overall conditioning.

Frequency: Three or four times a week

Mileage per walk: 3 to 5 miles

Long walk: 4 to 6 miles

Weekly mileage: 10 to 20 miles

For example, your walking days in the first week on your customized program might look like this:

	Sun	Mon	Tues	Wed	Thurs	Fri	Sat	Total miles
Week 1	Rest	Walk	Rest	Walk	Walk	Rest	Walk	12

Athletic Walking

As an athletic walker, you are already fit and active, and perhaps want to take your walking to the next level. This is all about "performance," whether you are competing only with yourself and your own abilities, with your friends, or even with runners in local races. Of course, it's also quite a bit about getting stronger and more fit.

Frequency: Five or six times a week

Mileage per walk: 4 to 6 miles

Long walk: 6 to 13 miles

Weekly mileage: 20 to 35 miles

For example, your walking days in the first week on your customized program might look like this:

	Sun	Mon	Tues	Wed	Thurs	Fri	Sat	Total miles
Week 1	Walk	Rest	Walk	Walk	Rest	Walk	Walk	25

Building Your Program

In addition to these guidelines, following a few helpful steps will help you fill in the blanks in your weekly and monthly program:

1. **Scheduling days to walk.** A few days before a new workout week begins, assess your schedule and responsibilities to decide when you can work out. Mark the days and times on a calendar. Writing them down will help you treat the workout like an appointment you can't miss and, therefore, scheduling them won't be left to chance. Following is an example:

	Sun	Mon	Tues	Wed	Thurs	Fri	Sat	Total miles
Week 1	Rest	Walk	Rest	Walk	Walk	Rest	Walk	

2. **Setting a goal.** Once you have scheduled the days, while remembering the hard–easy rule, think about what type of workout fits best on each day, considering your available time or other needs. If your goal is a particular weekly mileage, start with that total to determine how long each workout will be. Note that the total mileage goal has been included:

	Sun	Mon	Tues	Wed	Thurs	Fri	Sat	Total miles
Week 1	Rest	Walk	Rest	Walk	Walk	Rest	Walk	12

3. **Choosing workouts.** Now that your mileage is plugged in, pencil in the workouts you've been pondering. Include length, intensity, location, and time. These details have been added in the following chart:

	Sun	Mon	Tues	Wed	Thurs	Fri	Sat	Total miles
Week 1	Rest	MQ5	Rest	MS8	MS1	Rest	LS3	12
		3 miles Effort: 4-5 Neighbor-hood Early a.m.		3¼ miles Effort: 4 Neighbor-hood Evening	1¾ miles Effort: 3 Local mall Lunchtime		4 miles Effort: 5 City park	

Voila, your first week is done—just like paint by numbers! A blank four-week program template is on page 172 for you to copy as needed (see figure 13.1).

Conquering Life's Hurdles

Whether you run into a busy workweek, vacations, or bad weather, accomplishing your program can sometimes demand a few modifications. Never fear! Something is always better than nothing. That's where being flexible with your preferred workout time, location, and type can help you stick with a program. Putting together a workout schedule, then sticking to it, helps also. Then there are those times you travel—for fun, family, or business. Again, flexibility helps keep you healthy and on the path to fitness. Even learning how to cope with variations in weather and rehabilitation from a major or minor injury will keep the walker's smile on your face. It's all about flexibility. Read on.

Using a Treadmill

Even if you don't favor being inside, if the kids are home and need watching or it's snowing, you may need to hit the treadmill either at home or at a club. A treadmill can be a great tool. For more explanation about how to use them, refer to page 36 in chapter 4.

The most important thing to remember is that *any* workout can be done on a treadmill—just translate the minutes per mile to miles per hour using the chart on page 36. With that little bit of information, you can take any workout you had intended to do and accomplish it comfortably inside.

Here are other tips that will make your treadmill workout more comfortable:

- Keep a water bottle handy to keep you more comfortable in the often warmer, drier, and stuffier indoor air.
- Hang a small towel over the front rail or console so you can wipe your brow or hands, if you need to.
- If you go to a club, take a pair of water-resistant headphones because many have built-in systems for listening to radios or watching TV.
- If the lack of a breeze bothers you, set up a fan to blow on you, although some people may find that too chilly and simply prefer an open door or window.

Adjusting Your Schedule

Everybody has days or a week now and then when it seems impossible to squeeze in a workout. If you miss a workout, your program is not ruined. Doing a little something will help you stay on-track and it's better than nothing at all. Researchers have found that it takes three weeks on a limited schedule before you start to lose conditioning. So don't panic if your workout schedule sometimes has a few holes. If you must trim your schedule to accommodate interruptions, follow these guidelines to maintain fitness:

- **How often?** You can cut your workload by about a third without losing fitness. For example, if you normally work out every other day, aim for every third day, or two to three days a week.
- **How long?** Can't get in a 30- or 45-minute aerobic workout? Make it 15 or 20 minutes.
- **How hard?** When cutting back, skip the easy, dilly-dallying workouts. Instead make the most of your available time and concentrate on the more upbeat or more aerobically challenging workouts.

Taking Injuries in Stride

If you become injured and a strain or pain lasts more than a few days and limits your ability to exercise, you should consult a doctor or medical professional to find out what type of injury you have and how to treat it. Ignoring an injury, even one that seems minor, could set you up for additional injuries if you develop an imbalance in your gait or muscle tightness or weakness.

If you are recovering from an injury and working back into a walking program, don't start where you left off. Rather, step back into training with easier, shorter, less frequent walks. The rebuilding period should last as long as the time you were off. For example, if a calf strain kept you sidelined for two weeks, take two weeks to get back to where you were, even using cross-training workouts for less impact to start. If you are off for much longer, you may need to start back with a beginning program. In this case, consult your physician or a physical therapist to be sure you're resuming training at the proper level. Taking on too much, too soon—no matter how eager you are—could set you up for another injury. Slow and steady wins the race.

Coping With Weather

There is always weather. Sometimes pleasant and sometimes less pleasant, but weather happens and life goes on. Knowing what to expect and how to cope with it will make your program flow more smoothly. Use one of several national weather-oriented Web sites to track what's coming and going in your area. Many of these also track humidity, sunrise, sunset, smog levels, and barometric changes that might signal a storm. Some also have Doppler radar screens with moving pictures showing where storms are and how heavy they are. Local or cable television stations also provide weather forecasts.

Even unexpected weather doesn't have to keep you from a workout. Avoid being caught off-guard. Keep a workout bag at work in case an impending storm means you need to dash out at lunch or right after work. Or take your gear with you when running errands and go for a quick workout before heading home.

Use a trip to the club or a mall as options if the weather keeps you from walking outside. If you spend time at home either in a home office or with kids, be prepared to seize the moment between storms.

Shifting workout times as seasons change can help you stick to a walking program. You might want to get up early for a walk before it heats up in the summer, but on cooler spring or fall days, you might want to exercise in the late afternoon or evening. In the winter, a workout might be more comfortable at midday when it's warmest. Soon, you'll be playing hide-and-seek with the weather, making a game out of figuring out the best times for your workouts. Chapter 3 provides information on shoes and apparel so that you can gear up for the weather.

When winter weather strikes, don't be afraid to use it! Snowshoe, cross-country ski, or go for a winter-wonderland hike in waterproof shoes (with good tread for nonslip grip) on a packed trail or snow-covered street. Refer to additional information about cross-training in chapter 12.

What if it's summer and hot or smoggy? Head indoors or get out at the crack of dawn before the air heats up and ozone goes bad. Most metropolitan areas have some kind of official organization that issues advisories and information about air quality, sometimes even directly to your e-mail inbox if you sign up for them. Search the Internet to find one.

Armed with this book's training information and programs as your personal trainer, you will be well on your way to saying with pride, "Yes, I'm a walker!"

Sample Four-Week Program

	Sun	Mon	Tues	Wed	Thurs	Fri	Sat	Total miles
Week 1								
Week 2								
Week 3								
Week 4								

Figure 13.1 Program template.

Index

NOTE: Figures or tables are indicated by italicized *f,* or *t,* respectively, following page numbers.

About the Author

Therese Iknoian, MS, is an exercise physiologist, former nationally ranked race walker, and internationally published freelance health and fitness writer whose work has appeared in *Trail Runner*, *Men's Health*, *Fitness*, *Women's Day*, *Shape*, and *Parenting*, among others. She is also the cofounder and coeditor of the GearTrends Network with a Web site (GearTrends.com), trade magazines, and a news service (SNEWS) specializing in the outdoor, fitness, and sports markets.

As a race walker, Iknoian won numerous awards, including two silver medals at the 1993 and 1994 National Masters Track & Field Championships. In 1994, she broke the world record for her age group in the indoor 3-kilometer race walk.

Iknoian has authored two books on walking, *Fitness Walking* and *Walking Fast*, and has developed

walking and fitness programs for several international companies, including Polar, Nike, and Star Trac. She is a gold-certified instructor by the American Council on Exercise and is certified by the American College of Sports Medicine as a health and fitness instructor. She is a member of the IDEA association for fitness professionals and has been a featured presenter at past conventions.

Iknoian lives in the Sierra Nevada foothills of Northern California with her husband and fellow journalist, Michael Hodgson.